THE
OGRE

THE
OGRE

**Biography of a mountain
and the dramatic story
of the first ascent**

DOUG SCOTT

Leabharlanna Poibli Chathair Baile Átha Cliath
Dublin City Public Libraries

Vertebrate Publishing, Sheffield
www.v-publishing.co.uk

More books by Doug Scott

Big Wall Climbing (1974)
The Shishapangma Expedition (1984)
Himalayan Climber (1992)
Up and About (2015)

For more information about
Community Action Nepal, see:
www.canepal.org.uk

For Chris, Clive, Mo, Nick and Tut

THE OGRE
DOUG SCOTT

First published in 2017 by Vertebrate Publishing. Reprinted in 2017.

 Vertebrate Publishing
Crescent House, 228 Psalter Lane, Sheffield S11 8UT, United Kingdom.
www.v-publishing.co.uk

Front cover and frontispiece: The Ogre, Karakoram, Pakistan. Photo: Ronnie Richards.
Photography by Doug Scott unless otherwise credited.
Endpaper maps © Cyrille Levitte 2017.

This book is a work of non-fiction based on the life of Doug Scott. The author has stated
to the publishers that, except in such minor respects not affecting the substantial accuracy
of the work, the contents of the book are true.

A CIP catalogue record for this book is available from the British Library.

ISBN: 978-1-911342-79-3 (Hardback)
ISBN: 978-1-911342-80-9 (Ebook)

10 9 8 7 6 5 4 3 2

Every effort has been made to obtain the necessary permissions with reference to copyright
material, both illustrative and quoted. We apologise for any omissions in this respect
and will be pleased to make the appropriate acknowledgements in any future edition.

Design and production by
Jane Beagley, Vertebrate Publishing.

Hayloft Publishing Ltd completed the design, editing and typesetting of the first version of this book
By Way of ... The Ogre (ISBN 978-1-910237-37-3) to a print-ready stage. The right to publish and print this
version of this book has been transferred to Vertebrate Publishing.

Vertebrate Publishing is committed to printing on paper from sustainable sources.

Printed and bound in Scotland by Bell & Bain Ltd.

Contents

Preface

This book is a biography of the Ogre in two parts: the first part is concerned with the geological evolution and exploration from ancient times; the second part is more personal, covering the first ascent of the mountain and the drama of the descent with my two broken legs and Chris Bonington's smashed ribs.

The first section of the book involved a good deal of research that I found immensely interesting: I had been to many of the places the European explorers first saw, during eight visits to the Karakoram, the Central Hindu Kush of Afghanistan and Pik Lenin in the Pamirs. Without doubt most of what I have written has been said before, but not many can write it down so well and convincingly as Conway and Shipton, and, more recently, William Dalrymple and Rory Stewart.

This is to be the first of a series of books of a similar format. Over the next few years I intend to produce books about Kangchenjunga, Makalu, K2, Nanga Parbat, Everest and Baffin Island. The books will cover the exploration that first brought men to the mountains right up to the summit. To that extent these volumes will be innovative in that most books on mountain travel and exploration go no further than traversing the adjacent glaciers and crossing nearby cols. The climbing is from a different era – before satellite phones, the availability of accurate weather forecasts on a daily basis and before super-lightweight equipment and plastic boots filled with closed-cell foam.

This series will cover a golden age of British Himalayan climbing between 1970 and 1985. These were brilliant days when I, for one, could have gone from one expedition to the next without a break, pushing the limits of climbing rock at great altitude and to climb the highest mountains without bottled oxygen and some without fixed ropes in complete alpine style.

In the last year new material has become available to me – I came across a bundle of letters I had written to my wife and family during the expedition to the Ogre that I had not read since first writing them. Nick Estcourt's diary has become available since it is now lodged with the Mountain Heritage Trust;

Clive Rowland has made available his draft memoirs; and the 8mm film, together with supporting cassette tapes, have just been found by Jackie Anthoine forty years after Mo put them together.

I hope the reader will have a better understanding of those times and the part played in the climbs by my companions and the local villagers who helped us first reach the mountain and, in the case of the Ogre expedition, carried me down from it on a stretcher back to their village.

Each of the mountains I have climbed has been unique, presenting my friends and me with a new set of challenges every time. During the course of an expedition, and in overcoming these challenges, we became far more aware of ourselves and of each other. We were, for a time at least, able to return home wiser men, usually more at peace with ourselves and with more enthusiasm to do all that had to be done back home.

Introduction

The one man that stands out when thinking back to the British Ogre expedition to the Karakoram mountains in 1977 is the Balti porter, Taki, who, after carrying a twenty-five-kilogram box throughout a four-day approach march, over loose moraine and slippery glacier ice, produced from the folds of his shirts and smocks on arrival at Base Camp thirty-one eggs – none of which were even cracked. It is hard to know how he managed that but he did for only thirty rupees a day (£1.75).

There is no way any of our expedition could have walked over that shifting chaos of moraine rock, stumbled across bare ice and waded through soft snow without breaking such a cargo. Eight weeks later eight more Balti came up the Biafo Glacier to Base Camp and, with as much consideration as Taki had for his eggs, carried me down that same rough terrain with hardly a jolt to my broken legs.

Forty years later it suddenly seems appropriate to record the significant events that brought the Ogre into being, into human comprehension, right up to the summit, and how the descent was achieved with two smashed ribs and two broken legs.

Doug Scott
September 2017

PART **1**

1   **The Mountain**

The mighty Karakoram has within the range some of the highest mountains on the planet making it the most formidable of the mountain barriers dividing the Indian subcontinent from Central Asia. The rivers draining the southern flanks of the Karakoram flow into the Indus whereas those to the north are channelled into the Yarkand to eventually disappear into the parched deserts of Xinjiang. Aeons ago this part of the earth's surface was covered by an arm of the great Mesozoic Tethys Ocean that lay between the two contiguous continents of Gondwana and Laurasia containing all the land surface of the world. These two land masses split up, eventually forming the seven continents that exist today. I know this from reading Arthur Holmes' *Principles of Physical Geology* (1944) when at school and later a revised edition (1965) when teaching geography. More recently, *Colliding Continents* (2013) written by a good friend and Professor of Earth Sciences at Oxford, Mike Searle, has brought me up to date.

These prehistoric continents drifted about like surface clinker on the molten core of the earth, propelled by the convection currents rising up to the earth's mantle. Where two of these thermal currents came up together through the outer core and mantle to the surface and then diverged in opposite directions low mountains formed and tectonic plates were set in motion. Such activity still takes place on the ocean floor, as along the Mid-Atlantic Ridge, evidence of which is seen in Iceland. It is an island famous for its hot pools, geysers and dramatic volcanic activity sending huge plumes of ash into the atmosphere. It is also an island of increasing landmass as a result of the divergent, widening boundary between the North American tectonic plate and the Eurasian tectonic plate.

Movement of the continents resulted in an equal and opposite reaction where they collided, producing spectacular results. There the crust buckled

Left: The Ogre, the highest and most difficult peak in the area of the Biafo Glacier.
Photo: Galen Rowell, 1975.

Surtsey, the southernmost part of Iceland, is the furthest isle in this photograph. It erupted to the surface in 1963 and by 1967 reached its present size. It is an example of the submarine volcanic action coming up through the fissure of the sea floor known as the Mid-Atlantic Ridge.

and broke and was thrust up into huge mountain ranges. The drama is still in process in many parts of the world and none more so than in High Asia. Here the Indian plate, at the point of contact, was thrust beneath the Eurasian plate lifting Tibet to its current status – the highest plateau in the world. Further west, the result of one earth-shattering thrust after another was to produce corrugations in the form of a whole series of individual mountain ranges.

The modern-day rugby scrum provides a graphic analogy for colliding continents where one front row of muscular giants dips under the other to have to reform and push again, only next time both teams are so evenly matched the front rows rise up together. As the flow of the game is brought to a halt yet again, both teams push against each other, only now to swivel round and break from each other at which point the referee blows the whistle for this infringement or fault. The first stoppage we can equate to the subduction of the Indian plate under Tibet; the second to the great continental collision along the Himalaya; and the third to the formation of huge strike-slip faults like the Karakoram fault, Kunlun or Altyn Tagh faults in Tibet, along which continental plates have moved laterally against each other.

Right in the centre of all this activity at the 'Roof of the World' are the Pamirs, known to geographers as the 'Pamir Knot', from whence radiate out north-east the Tien Shan, south-east the Karakoram and Kunlun, south-west the Hindu Kush and the Pamir range itself to the west. South of the Karakoram, and running parallel to it, is the Ladakh range below which is the Indus River separating both the Karakoram and the Ladakh range from the western end

Great Trango Tower: first climbed in 1977 by Americans Dennis Hennek, Jim Morrissey, John Roskelley, Galen Rowell and Kim Schmitz.

of the great Himalayan range. The extent of the Himalaya is defined as lying between Nanga Parbat in the west and Namcha Barwa in the east.

The Himalaya is the longest of all the mountain ranges of Asia, but the greatest concentration of high mountains are north from the western end of the Himalaya. These mountains are the youngest and are still rising under the pressure of the Indian plate that for the last fifty-five million years has been pushing inexorably against the Eurasian plate. This is happening at an average rate of five centimetres per annum as the mountains along the line of contact are still rising, outpacing erosion by about seven millimetres annually.

This concept corresponds with the beliefs and mythologies of the people that now inhabit these mountains. Tibetan cosmology has it that the land (Mount Meru) emerged from a primeval ocean, and in the Hindu epic *Mahabharata* reference is also made to the watery origins of the Himalayan mountains. It is not easy to visualise geological time but we are reminded of it every few years when this mountain building manifests spectacularly in the form of catastrophic earthquakes and frequent tremors causing landslip, avalanche, the destruction of towns and villages, and the deaths of hundreds, sometimes thousands, of mountain people.

The folded sedimentary and metamorphic rocks making up the majority of the newly formed mountain ranges of the world were later penetrated by massive injections of molten granites in the form of batholiths. These intrusions of magma cooled slowly within the country rock to form igneous rocks, the main one being granite. Over millions of years the granite is exposed to the surface as the overlying rock is removed through the process of erosion.

Left: The Nameless Tower. First climbed in 1976 by Martin Boysen and Mo Anthoine, and by Joe Brown and Martin Howells the following day.

Above: Excellent granite for rock climbing on Lobsang Spire. *Photo:* Greg Child.

The granite itself is then subject to all the forces of nature, the wind and the rain and, in particular high in the mountains, the mechanical weathering of freezing and thawing, of glaciation and denudation by rivers loaded with grit and stone. The roughness of granite is due to the resistance of the quartz to decay. It has become the most cherished rock for climbing as it provides such good friction for hand and foot. Not only is this hard, rough granite an ideal medium for climbing, it tends to erode into shapely spires and formidable towers with huge rock walls that add to the challenge and satisfaction of reaching their summits. Just as the Western Alps have given rise to Mont Blanc granite and the famous Chamonix Aiguilles, so has the granite of the Karakoram eroded into the Baltoro spires and the Latok mountains, the highest of which is Baintha Brakk, known to the climbing world as the Ogre.

The Karakoram is considered to be the loftiest mountain range of all, with the highest concentration of peaks over 26,000 feet (7,900 metres) giving the range an average height of 6,100 metres / 20,000 feet, along its 300-mile length. Another interesting statistic is that there are more than sixty peaks above 7,000 metres (23,000 feet) dotted about the Karakoram. They are the most spectacular and awe-inspiring mountains imaginable; they are literally breathtaking when they first impress themselves upon the eye.

The name Karakoram seems to have originally been applied to the range by merchants crossing over what is now the Karakoram Pass. The word *kara* in the Turkic language is the common word for black and *kurum* is the everyday word for stones as used to this day throughout Central Asia.

There is some logic in this since there are large areas of loose black shale lying all around the Karakoram Pass. The fact that the indigenous population, deep in these mountains, now call them the Karakoram is probably a result of the Survey of India adopting the name when first surveying the peaks in the mid-nineteenth century.

Tom Longstaff makes a valid point in his book *This My Voyage* (1950):

> It is to be regretted that Karakoram is now the official spelling of this name. The mistake probably arose from following the rules for translation of Urdu into English. But the word is of the Turki language of Central Asia, and not Urdu. The name of the ancient capital of the Mughal Turks in distant Mongolia always has been and still is written Karakorum.

The only slight advantage of having it Karakoram is that it delineates the mountain from the ancient town.

The range is situated much further from the equator than the central Himalaya of Nepal. The highest mountain in the Karakoram, K2 (35 degrees 52' N), is nearly eight degrees north of Everest (27 degrees 59' N). The climate as a consequence is more severe with glaciation reaching down to lower altitudes than in the central Himalaya. Four of the largest glaciers outside of the polar regions wind their way down through the granite rocks of the Karakoram. There is the Siachen, forty-five miles long to the south-east of the range. Further west the Baltoro, including the Godwin-Austen Glacier, flows down from Windy Gap and Skyang Kangri for thirty-six miles. Again moving further west there are the Hispar and Biafo glaciers which are only separated by the icy Hispar Pass. Together they provide a continuous highway of seventy-six miles on ice and snow, making it the longest such journey outside the polar regions. Right at the north-west end of the Karakoram is the thirty-five-mile-long Batura Glacier, west of the Hunza River and the Karakoram Highway, that has dramatically opened up the region to coach loads of tourists.

There is a considerable climatic difference between the Everest region of Nepal and the Karakoram, not only because of the distance from the equator but also on account of K2 being at least 900 miles from the ocean and any maritime influence, whereas Everest is only 400 miles from the Bay of Bengal and receives the full force of the monsoon. K2 and the surrounding area on the other hand receives a diminished attenuated monsoon whereby much of the moisture is dissipated over the foothills and sub-Himalayan mountains before reaching the Karakoram.

Right: On the Karakoram Highway with the huge North Face of Rakaposhi dominating the Hunza valley.

2 Ancient History of Exploration

It was only during the last 200 years that the outside world came to know of the glaciers and the complex topography of the Karakoram. It is difficult, even now, to contemplate Karakoram geography without reference to modern-day maps. Two centuries ago there were no maps, only fragments of information gathered locally by itinerant travellers. Travel always was, for those who lived there, difficult and dangerous, for down in the valley bottom were raging torrents above which there were frequent landslides and avalanches of snow in winter. Crossing high passes remains to this day a challenge due to the problems of altitude. The valleys were so isolated that communities long ago divided into separate kingdoms, speaking different languages and often at war with each other. The villagers in their isolation always seemed suspicious of foreigners, especially those who came in from 'over the mountains' for they could reveal to enemies in other valleys unprotected ways to enter and rape and pillage.

There is a useful reference to the early history of this region in the *Pakistan Trekking Guide*. It is written by Isobel Shaw and her son, Ben, and is one of the most comprehensive trekking guides ever produced. Six thousand years ago there were hunters and herders in the mountains of northern Pakistan. In the eighteenth century BC the Aryans invaded the north of Pakistan to fight battles in the Swat valley. The high mountains of Asia were not only known to the ancients but also alluded to in Indian mythologies and with some accuracy as to their alignment. In the *Mahabharata* the Pandavas journey over small mountains, outer mountains and inner mountains corresponding to the sub-Himalayan foothills, lesser or middle Himalaya and the Great Himalaya on the watershed we know of today.

In the sixth century BC Darius the Great of Persia conquered the northern part of Pakistan. Three centuries later the Greeks gained first-hand knowledge of the Hindu Kush and possibly Baltistan as a result of Alexander the Great and his Macedonian invasion of India. Persian, Greek and also Roman scholars have all referred to the high mountains in the region of the

Ulugh Beg (1394–1449), one of Islam's greatest astronomers and mathematicians during the Middle Ages. He was the grandson of the great warrior Tamerlane.

Karakoram and have them stretching from west to east and they are actually drawn with that alignment by Ptolemy on the map of the world he produced in the second century.

Following on from the Greeks the next major influence upon this region of Central Asia was the increase in trade from east to west on a route that became known as the Silk Road. The ever-increasing trade, mainly in silk, began in China during the Han Dynasty (206 BC to AD 220) with Chinese merchants bringing their goods into central Asia to be moved on by middlemen. These entrepreneurial brokers were mainly Scythians and later Parthians, both of whom prospered from receiving and passing on merchandise to ancient Rome.

There was never any one single highway; no M1 across Asia into Europe, no single line of communication such as the Trans-Siberian railway that today connects the whole of northern Eurasia. The Silk Road was more like a wide corridor of scattered trading centres with offshoots north and south. One main route south went over the Karakoram Pass to Leh, Lahore and the Arabian Sea route to Mesopotamia and the Mediterranean. With the exchange of goods came cultural connectivity and the spread of ideas, inventions, religion, art and people themselves.

This global trade ebbed and flowed according to circumstance for it was always at the mercy of climate change, famine, war, economic reverses and,

Above: Ulugh Beg's observatory, Samarkand. His work in trigonometry and spherical geometry contributed indirectly to the Great Trigonometrical Survey of India.

Top, opposite page: The Registan is at the heart of the ancient city of Samarkand, now in Uzbekistan. It was one of the most important places on the Silk Road.

Bottom, opposite page: The Satpara Buddha: the Buddha was carved into the granite and it is estimated it was made in the seventh century. It is to be found halfway between Skardu and Satpara.

during the 1340s, the Black Death. This disease appears to have originated in Central Asia and so quickly spread along the Silk Road to eventually devastate Europe, where at least one third of the population perished.

By the second century AD the Kushan empire was well established in the north-west of India and the Pamir mountains where it had control of the lucrative trade in silk. The Kushans, who were Buddhist, established a winter capital at Peshawar. The most famous Kushan king, Kanishka (ruled AD c.128–151), built innumerable monasteries and stupas all around the upper Indus valley, and in the environs of Gilgit, Hunza and Chitral particularly at the summit of various passes.

The Chinese embraced Buddhism in the first century AD. Thereafter Chinese monks made arduous pilgrimages into Tibet, the Himalaya and Karakoram. One of the main pilgrim routes went through Kashgar, over the Boroghil and Darkot passes to Swat. Faxian made this journey in AD 403

writing a detailed description of his travels which took a whole month from Kashgar to Darel. Hsuan-Tsang (AD 602–664) travelled for sixteen years through the entire length of the Himalaya keeping complete records for his book *Datang-Xiyu-Ji* ('Great Tang Dynasty Record of the Western Regions').

Many of the early travellers came to honour the most important of all Buddhist shrines in the region – the thirty-metre-high wooden statue of Maitreya Bodhisattva. The land around Darel and the Swat valley was fertile enough to support a large community of monks. It was from there that Guru Rinpoche, known also as Padmasambhava, the most revered of all the Buddhist missionaries, left the valley of Swat in the eighth century to spread Buddhism amongst the Tibetans. Until the eighth century anyone travelling through Tibet required a large military escort. After Guru Rinpoche's conversion of the people to Buddhism, and with a rejuvenation of the Bon religion, peace reigned.

3 European Interest in the Region

Western Europeans became more interested in the far east of Asia after the arrival of the Mongol hordes in Eastern Europe. Plenipotentiaries had been sent by the Pope and the King of Hungary to make contact with the Great Khan then ruling his empire from the town of Karakorum (Harhorin) to the west of present-day Ulan Bator. Louis IX of France despatched a messenger, the Flemish monk and traveller William of Rubruck, on a fact-finding mission (1253–1255); on his return William reported the presence of a French female cook, a German silversmith and the nephew of an English bishop. The court and town was a bustle of commercial activity with people from all parts of the empire and beyond, engaged in trade but also in serious open debate. There were not only mosques but there was also a Christian church. His report tempered the entrenched European opinion that the Tatars were all barbarians.

Nearly 750 years ago Niccolo and Maffeo Polo left Venice for a second visit to the Great Khan, this time accompanied by Niccolo's son, seventeen-year-old Marco. They travelled through Herat and Bokhara (Bukhara) on the Silk Road, north of the Pamirs and north of the Karakoram mountains, passing through Samarkand, Kashgar (Kashi), Yarkand (Shache) and Khotan (Hotan). They were the guests of Kublai Khan from 1275 to 1292. Marco was a particularly welcome guest due to his flair for languages and administrative skills.

The Mughal capital had been relocated to Dadu (Beijing) with a summer palace at Xanadu. The family travelled widely around the realm until finally they were allowed to leave China in a flotilla of fourteen junks bound for Hormuz in Persia. Two years after leaving the Great Khan they were back home in Venice. Marco's triumphant return was short-lived for while fighting for Venice against Genoa during a naval battle he was captured and imprisoned where his memoirs were recorded.

Although Marco had penetrated deep into the heart of the Mongol soul and way of life he wasn't the only European to journey east as William of

Crossing the Indus upstream from Skardu.

Rubruck revealed. There were many others who, no doubt, had interesting tales to tell. It is the old story that, if you are to be famous, then you must write books or have books written about you! As luck would have it for Marco and for us he was imprisoned with Rustichello of Pisa, a well-known author of romantic novels, who, over the three years of their incarceration, wrote up Marco's account of his remarkable journey east and the time he spent with the Great Khan. The Western world had the benefit of Marco's observations made within the Great Khan's inner circle. These revelations in his book, *Travels,* helped to bring the educated elite of Europe closer to the Far East and encourage others to emulate such ventures.

Marco made very little reference to the Karakoram and no reference at all to their name. The first Europeans to travel into the high mountains of Asia were the Jesuit missionaries based in Goa. During the seventeenth and eighteenth centuries they came in search of Prester John, a legendary Christian patriarch and king popular in European chronicles, following up on rumours, subsequently found to be false, that there were enclaves of Nestorian Christians practising their religion in the Himalaya and Tibet. Portuguese traders had long ago reported, on their return to Goa, that up in the Himalaya they had heard that the inhabitants were practising their religion with all the trappings of a Catholic church service. What their informants had actually witnessed was the Buddhists practising their faith, swinging incense, lighting candles and chanting traditional incantations.

This came to light only after the journeys made throughout the region by a Portuguese Jesuit, Bento de Goes, in 1603, who joined a trading caravan from Lahore to Kabul, and later through the Pamirs to Yarkand. In doing so he became the first European to cross from India over the mountains into Central Asia. In 1624 courageous Catholic priests Father Antonio de Andrade and Brother Manuel Marques made a difficult four-month journey from Agra, crossing the 18,000-foot Mana Pass, to arrive in Tsaparang on the Upper Sutlej. It was there they established a mission, subsequently visited by many other Jesuits, some via the Mana Pass but others through Kulu and over the Rohtang Pass further to the east.

Ippolito Desideri (1684–1733) will for ever be associated with the early explorations of Tibet. To know more about this it is worth referring to the comprehensive *An Account of Tibet – The Travels of Ippolito Desideri of Pistoia,* edited by Filippo de Filippi (1931). Early on in his travels Desideri became the first known European to have crossed the Zoji La when, in 1715, he journeyed from Srinagar in the Vale of Kashmir to Leh in Ladakh. Missionary necessity enabled him to overcome his horror of travelling into the mountains since he found them 'the very picture of desolation, horror and death itself'. Almost a century later, at the end of the eighteenth century, Westerners began to romanticise the mountains and hold them as places also for spiritual renewal.

4   **The East India Company**

Following the defeat of the Spanish Armada in 1588, London merchants petitioned Queen Elizabeth I for permission and support to trade in the Indian Ocean and beyond. Despite losing ships, the merchant adventurers persisted with their plans, and on the last day of 1600 the Queen granted a royal charter to the 'Governor and Company of Merchants of London Trading into the East Indies'. Convoys of merchant ships made huge profits for the merchants and their aristocratic backers who were able to establish sprawling country estates on the proceeds of their profits. The company became known as the East India Company and also as the Honourable or British East India Company and informally as the John Company, after merchant and ship owner Sir John Watts, one of the company's founders who was elected its governor in April 1601.

The East India Company expanded to account for half the world's trade in basic commodities, such as silk, cotton, indigo dye, tea, opium and saltpetre, used in the manufacture of gunpowder, after seeing off the Portuguese, Dutch and finally the French. During the first 100 years it was primarily a trading company with the governors reluctant to spend profits building an empire. However, with the establishment of trading posts, the defeat of a Mughal viceroy in 1757 at the Battle of Plassey in Benghal, and with the general decline of the Mughal empire in India, the company expanded the territory it controlled.

By 1803 the East India Company had built up a private army of more than a quarter of a million troops which at the time was twice the size of the British Army. The company increasingly took over administration for the territories it had moved into until the Indian Mutiny of 1857. The following year the Government of India Act passed through parliament enabling the British Crown to take direct control of Indian affairs. The British involvement in India moved on a stage into the British Raj.

Commerce, the defence of empire, as well as missionary zeal, helped people to overcome fears of the snowy ranges. Servants of the East India

Company were sent north to unravel the complexities of the geography so that trading routes might be established through the mountain barrier to the fabled cities on the silk route. Increasingly the East India Company and the British Government sought information about the topography as well as the inhabitants of the mountainous North-West Frontier so as to be prepared for incursions by Russian and even French aggressors.

In 1798, 40,000 French troops sailed from Toulon and Marseille for Egypt in preparation to take back India from the British. The governor general of India, Lord Wellesley, used this opportunity to embark upon a 'forward policy' by taking control of most of India except Sind, the Punjab and Kashmir, all of which remained independent kingdoms. This was a remarkable achievement in his seven years tenure as governor general. However, by then Nelson had destroyed all but two vessels of the French fleet lying off the coast of Egypt.

Despite this setback Napoleon kept alive the possibility of driving the British out of India and creating a French empire in the east. In 1807, full of confidence from recent victories in Europe, he suggested to Tsar Alexander I of Russia that the French and the Russians should combine to attack India from the north. Napoleon was prepared to contribute 50,000 troops. The East India Company and the British Government had heard many rumours about Russian designs on India which had largely been discounted due to the distances involved and the harsh terrain that would have to be crossed, but now, with the support of a military genius, the company was galvanised into action.

Napoleon's adventures in Egypt suddenly alerted the British to the vulnerability of their Indian empire and how important it was to steer Persia and Afghanistan away from having any dealings with the French or the Russians. Napoleon had set the foreign policy agenda where India was concerned for the next 150 years.

The most likely route the French and Russian invasion would take was in the footsteps of Alexander, overland through Persia and into Afghanistan or Baluchistan. Overtures were therefore made to the shah of Persia who eventually came firmly under British influence thanks to Captain John Malcolm, a native of Eskdale in Dumfriesshire. This young soldier from the Borders was by 1810 more knowledgeable of Persia than any other Briton. Part of the arrangement made with the shah for his support of Britain was that the British would help train his army in modern warfare. Malcolm, who had by now been promoted to major general, came with a small group of highly trained officers to not only instruct the Persian army but also to check out and report back on the geography of Persia from a military perspective.

Nanga Parbat: this magnificent mountain delineates the western end of the Himalayan range.

The next step was more hazardous, requiring secret incursions into other more hostile states to the north and south of Persia. All this is well written up in Peter Hopkirk's book *The Great Game*. There the reader will know of the valiant efforts during 1810 of Captain Charles Christie and Lieutenant Henry Pottinger of the 5th Bombay Native Infantry. Both young men, barely in their twenties, were tasked to go where no European had gone before, through challenging terrain forever at the mercy of fickle and hostile tribal chiefs.

They had parted company in Nushki in Baluchistan to widen the scope of their reconnaissance; Charles Christie eventually entered Herat, western Afghanistan. He was only the second European to venture into this important town, strategically placed on the historic east–west route connecting Turkey, Iran and Afghanistan with the Indus valley. Pottinger travelled further west and eventually after three months, and more than 2,250 miles later, they were both together in Isfahan. They could now finally relax in friendly Persia, being out of danger from hostile tribesmen, and write up reports that proved to be invaluable to the British defence of India from the west. They had managed to evade capture by disguising themselves variously as holy men or as Tatar horse dealers. Such men, so resourceful and able to think on their feet, were the backbone of empire at this time, with more to follow in their footsteps.

As late as 1829, Lord Ellenborough, the president of the East India Company Board of Control, suggested, according to Charles Masson, the army deserter who became a government spy in Kabul, 'We ought to have "information". The first, second and third thing a government always ought to have is information.' To this end there were fifteen confirmed Europeans on fact-finding missions into Afghanistan before the first Afghan War of 1839. One of the most effective of these agents was Mountstuart Elphinstone (1779–1859) who was in 1809 the first envoy to the court of Kabul.

By 1815 he had published, in two volumes, *An Account of the Kingdom of Caubul,* which, apart from a huge amount of detail covering the social and economic life of the people, also included a map of 'Caubul On A Reduced Scale Shewing Its Relative Situation To The Neighbouring Countries'. The map featured 'The Kurrakooram' and the 'Hemalleh' as well as the major river systems of the area showing the Indus flowing through Kashmir. This was the first detailed map of the north-west Indian subcontinent. The map was of considerable use to future travellers and the book their bible for the next fifty years.

Elphinstone was born in Dumbarton and after an education at the Edinburgh Royal High School, joined the civil service of the East India Company arriving in Calcutta in 1796. He not only distinguished himself collecting information in Afghanistan but also impressed his superiors, including Wellesley, for having a natural aptitude for soldiering. He became governor of Bombay where he put his energy and negotiating skills into establishing education for Indians at a time when educating 'natives' was held in horror back in Britain. Elphinstone College, which he established in 1856, is a fitting legacy to his philanthropic endeavours. Another legacy was to have built the first bungalow on the Malabar Hill of Bombay. It quickly became, and remains, the upmarket residential area of the city where the former editor of the *Himalayan Journal* and secretary of the Himalayan Club lives.

The Franco-Russian attack never took place since France set about Russia and lost an army during the retreat in midwinter from a burnt-out Moscow. The Russians, emboldened by their success in reducing La Grande Armée from 400,000 to 9,000, again turned their attentions towards the East and the Indian subcontinent.

The springs to adventure might be narrowed down to man's propensity for being inquisitive but also acquisitive. It was Cicero in the first century BC who observed 'What has always fascinated man the most is the unknown'.

This fascination surely must underlie one of the main reasons men left hearth and home to face unimaginable hardship and frustrations, sometimes over many years, journeying through the Karakoram and surrounding mountain ranges. Ostensibly, they may well have gone as geographers opening up routes for trade or defence, but they were also smitten with the addiction to the uncertainties of the unknown.

During the first half of the nineteenth century several brave and resourceful Europeans arrived on the scene, including William Moorcroft (1767–1825). To all outward appearances he explored the Karakoram and beyond out of commercial interest. He became obsessed with opening up trade with Central Asia between Yarkand and the Caspian Sea to ensure the protection of British India in depth by creating trading posts throughout the region. John Keay in *When Men & Mountains Meet* (1977) summed up his vision as 'bringing prosperity and order whilst making of the region an outer rampart in the landward defences of India'.

Moorcroft was from Ormskirk in Lancashire and became a veterinary surgeon later employed by the East India Company in Bengal. During his time in India and Central Asia Moorcroft successfully investigated opportunities to develop a trade in wool with Tibet. In doing so he introduced wool from Tibetan goats that could be made into fine pashmina shawls. He is also credited with discovering the true source of the Indus and Sutlej and was thus able to prove they were quite separate from the Ganges river systems. Moorcroft also plotted on his map the Yarkand River and showed for the first time that it rises on the north flank of the Karakoram mountains. He was the first Englishman into Leh from where he made incursions into the Karakoram exploring the Nubra Valley at the eastern end of the range. He was regarded by his contemporaries, and later by Kenneth Mason, as one of the most important explorers of the region and, like so many, his life ended tragically still in harness in the service of the company.

From 1819 to 1825 Moorcroft travelled into Ladakh, Kashmir, Baltistan and Afghanistan where he eventually died in mysterious circumstances, possibly from a fever. However, his travelling companions, George Guthrie, George Trebeck and Moorcroft's regular interpreter, perished at the same time also from unknown causes suggesting they may well have been murdered for their possessions or, as rumour would have it at the time, poisoned by Russian agents. Fortunately, Moorcroft's papers were discovered and published in 1841, including a map, drawn up with the aid of a sketch made by George Trebeck.

Here, of course, use of the word 'discover' is in relative terms: it is not as in making discoveries in Antarctica where no one had ever been before; discoveries here invariably mean 'seen for the first time by non-indigenous

The Deosai Plateau: crossing the Parishing river in 1985.

inhabitants'. The fact that Moorcroft spent years travelling as far as Bokhara in Uzbekistan looking for better stud horses to improve the bloodline of East India Company horses suggests that sheer curiosity to look around the next corner was a major motivating factor. In fact, he didn't find any of the horses he was looking for in Bokhara but he did find considerable evidence of Russian penetration all along the Silk Road and to the north of the Karakoram.

In the book *When Men & Mountains Meet* the reader discovers that when Moorcroft first alerted the authorities in India of the Russian presence in the Trans Himalaya, the reaction of the East India Company and the British Government was lukewarm. They started to take far more interest in the mapping of the north-western end of the Himalaya and the Karakoram mountains only when it became ever-more evident the Russians had not only commercial aspirations, but also designs to make political capital in the Indian subcontinent.

Alexander Burnes (1805–1841) from Montrose in Scotland was the first major player in the Great Game who took up the baton from Moorcroft to march into the north-west highlands of the subcontinent and on into Afghanistan. Appropriately it was Burnes who, in 1832 on his way to Bokhara, found Moorcroft's grave on the outskirts of Balkh. Burnes, the first cousin of Robert Burns the poet, went out to India at the age of sixteen. He first joined the East India Company army, during which time he became fluent in Hindi,

Urdu and Farsi and worked as an interpreter. He also developed a keen interest in the geography and history of north-west India.

In 1831 he managed to inveigle his way on to an expedition to explore the Indus. King William IV wished to give a present of five English dray horses to Ranjit Singh who had previously presented King William with fine Kashmiri shawls. The Sikhs, under their able ruler, Ranjit Singh, had built up a strong kingdom in the Punjab, following the downfall of the Mughals. Ranjit Singh managed to coexist with the British without serious problem.

The British had long since established friendly relations with Ranjit and, in fact, after he conquered Kashmir in 1817, he had allowed the British to explore Ladakh, Kashmir and Baltistan. However, the British were alarmed to hear that Ranjit was exploring the possibility of commercial contracts with the Russians and had sent an envoy to St Petersburg. Finally, after Ranjit Singh's death, the British Government decided to follow Moorcroft's advice to see if the Indus river was navigable not only for trade but also to move troops whenever it was necessary to keep order and the Russians at bay.

Lord Ellenborough was convinced that the Russian advance had to be stopped well before it poured into the Indus valley. The native population might well take advantage of such a conflict with the Russians within India as an opportunity to rebel against British domination. Without reliable maps Ellenborough knew any military campaign would be seriously handicapped.

He hit upon the idea to persuade the maharajah that the only reasonable way to deliver the horses to Lahore was not over 700 miles of difficult and baking hot countryside but by river boat. Burnes was chosen to lead the expedition as it was recognised that he had exceptional qualities. Already, at the age of twenty-five, he was not only fluent in three local languages but he also had an ear for dialect. He was slight of build but brimming with self-confidence and determination, and yet, at the same time, had a great deal of charm. He quickly rose through the ranks of the 1st Bombay Light Infantry to be transferred to the prestigious Indian Political Service. They sailed from Kutch in January 1831, together with five horses and a newly made gilded state coach built in Bombay.

William Dalrymple has written an excellent introduction to a recent edition of Burnes's book, *Travels into Bohkara* (edited by Kathleen Hopkirk). Dalrymple notes the 'five huge dapple-grey Suffolk dray horses being punted peacefully up river' to the amazement of the Punjabis who though fanatical horsemen had never seen anything like 'the little English elephants' before. Burnes delivered the cargo to a very appreciative maharajah and details of the river and surroundings to Government of India intelligence. During the following years he continued journeying through Afghanistan, Bokhara and Persia as the eyes and ears of empire, all of which was written up in his book first published in 1835. It became an instant bestseller in England with 900 copies sold on the first day of publishing. He became something of a celebrity and, after his violent death, a national hero.

Such were his diplomatic skills that Burnes was sent on a political mission to Kabul to gather information on the mishmash of tribal loyalties and to offer not only facts, but also advice so that the Government of India could formulate an effective policy. Unfortunately, Burnes' advice was overruled and the first Afghan War broke out in 1839 ending disastrously in 1842 with 4,500 British and Indian troops killed along with some 12,000 camp followers. During this period, with the 4,500 troops camped half an hour away, a mob attacked Burnes in his residence as they held him responsible for the British encroachment into their country.

The British Army, under the vacillating command of Major General William Elphinstone, left their decision to help Burnes too late. He and his brother Charles were hacked to pieces. A year later in 1842 all but a few of the Indian Army had been decimated on their retreat back towards the Indus valley. Traditionally, history has it that only the assistant surgeon, William Brydon, reached Jalalabad on 13 January 1842 to relate the slaughter. There were a number of sepoy survivors who had hidden in caves and managed to trickle back to the Indus valley. There were also hostages that were later released after a retaliatory attack on Kabul and into Bamian Province by General George Pollock and General William Nott.

The British policy makers either failed to realise or, more likely, chose to ignore that Afghanistan would always be more of a liability than a beneficial buffer state. Their spies had let their superiors know Afghanistan was not a stable, single entity with an overall central power structure. Readers of Rory Stewart's journey off the beaten track across Afghanistan, will find in his book *The Places In Between* that to this day, as the title suggests, Afghanistan and its people are not as anywhere else.

It is the fate of the people born upon the 'Roof of the World' that their land was coveted and attacked from prehistory onwards. It is impossible not to admire the spirit of this country made up of mountain dynasties, all fiercely independent, consisting of mountain warriors up in the clouds, well versed in manipulating the invaders crowding their space. Yet the British, followed by the Russians and now the Americans, have moved in on the country forgetting the lessons of history, giving some credence to Marx's observation that history repeats itself 'first as tragedy, then as farce'.

The Great Game, as immortalised by Kipling in his novel *Kim*, was to prove a deadly game for many. The year after Burnes perished so did Captain Arthur Conolly who, according to Peter Hopkirk, was the first to coin the name 'Great Game'. While trying to secure the release of his brother officer,

Godfrey Thomas Vigne (1801–1863).

Colonel Charles Stoddart, in June 1842, both Conolly and Studdart were beheaded under the orders of the Emir of Bokhara.

Godfrey Vigne (1801–1863) from Walthamstow, then in Essex, an Harrovian, barrister, county cricketer and considerable artist, travelled extensively between 1835 and 1838 throughout Kashmir and Ladakh. His family were wealthy merchants who supplied the East India Company with gunpowder. He became the first European to describe Nanga Parbat which he did after crossing the Gurais Pass in 1835 en route to Baltistan. He was quite smitten when 'the stupendous peak of Diarmul, or Nungu Purbut, more than forty miles distant, in a straight line, but appearing to be much nearer, burst upon my sight'.

A week later after crossing the undulating Deosai Plateau he marched down into the Indus valley and became the first foreigner to enter Skardu. There are suggestions that the Macedonian Greeks had been in the region in 320 BC. Alexander himself did reach the valley of Swat, but whether or not his troops explored the valleys to the east as far as Skardu is open to question. The suggestion that they did is based on the town's name possibly deriving

Looking north to the Indus and Shigar valleys from the northern edge of the Deosai Plateau.

from Iskandariya which is the Balti rendering of Alexander. A short distance upstream from Skardu there is the Indus ferry. The inflated buffalo and goat skin barges are known locally as 'Alexander's Barge'.

Vigne wrote of his travels in these mountain ranges in his classic *Travels in Kashmir* (1842). His writing portrays a man as interested in appreciating the mountains as a means to lift his spirits rather than just a physical challenge to pass through. By the late eighteenth century attitudes began to change towards the mountains; this change continued into the nineteenth century when Ruskin noted in his *Modern Painters* (1856) that 'Mountain gloom gave way to mountain glory'. Vigne was not only one of the first to describe the mountains in romantic terms but also by 1838 he had established and then informed the Western world that the Karakoram was every bit as formidable as the Himalaya with huge glacier systems never before known or visited.

In 1835 he walked from Skardu up to the snout of the Chogolungma Glacier that is aligned parallel to the Hispar. Vigne wrote of the Basho river issuing from the glacier out of a cave in the ice cliff a hundred feet high and a quarter of a mile wide; it was 'no insignificant brook, but a large and ready formed river' roaring down its rocky bed towards the Shigar river and the Indus.

This first visit to Skardu by a foreigner was quickly followed by a second when, a few months later, the Scottish doctor and adventurer John Henderson entered Skardu in October 1835. He had followed the Indus down from Leh, dressed in native attire, all tattered and torn by the time he returned to Srinagar, where he was able to compare notes with Vigne.

5 Scottish Contribution to Empire

In the summer of 1838, Hugh Falconer, with the support of Rajah Ahmud Shah, traced the Shigar branch of the Indus to its source in the glacier on the southern flank of the 'Mooztagh' range. Having examined the 'great glaciers of a Arindoh [Arandu] and of the Braldoh [Braldu] valley' he returned to the Punjab via Astore, plant hunting as he went. Falconer is rarely mentioned in the various accounts of Karakoram exploration such as those by John Keay, despite being possibly the first foreigner to discover the Biafo Glacier, cross the Skaro La to pass through Askole and reach the Baltoro Glacier.

Falconer was born in a leap year on 29 February 1808 at Forres, on the banks of the Mosset river, and was, significantly perhaps, the youngest of seven children. He was a brilliant pupil at the local Forres Grammar School where he developed a lifetime's passion for natural history, particularly geology and botany. After a classic Scottish further education, studying both literature and science at Aberdeen University he then turned to medicine receiving an MD from Edinburgh University in 1829. He proceeded to India as an assistant surgeon in the service of the East India Company but within a year was unravelling the mysteries of Indian geology and discovering, recording and collecting not only rocks and fossils but also native plants.

At his death on 31 January 1865 it was written:

> There was but one feeling among men of science – that a master-mind had passed away and left little behind of the vast amount of palaeontological knowledge acquired during a period of thirty years – having a natural aversion to publish views without thoroughly sifting every fact which could be brought forward to corroborate or refute them.

Yet another Scot, Thomas Thomson, distinguished himself – this time by being the first to spend a winter in Skardu as he did in 1847. He was working for the Boundary Commission but he was also an exhaustive botanist and collector of plants. He was one of the lucky ones at the time to survive the rigours of India and, in his case, to end his days happily working at Kew Gardens and recognised as one of the greatest botanists of his day. Few of the explorers of High Asia's mountains, rocks, flora and fauna lived past the age of retirement, such were the rigours of the terrain through which they had passed. So many young men, especially from Scotland, intelligent and highly educated, resilient and incredibly resourceful, achieved so much in the service of empire.

The Scots were mainly responsible for a more liberal form of British imperialism. The empire would always be, at heart, of strategic and commercial benefit to Britain. That did not prevent the idea growing that Britain should, in the words of Rudyard Kipling, take on 'the white man's burden' and also run the country for its own good. The new mood had little to do with saving souls for a Christian God but all about improving the lot of the native population materially, by putting in better roads and schools, creating an impartial justice system and generally lifting the standard of living. This humane imperialism was ushered in as a result of the East India Company commissioning James Mill to write *The History of British India* (1817) – the company got more than they bargained for.

Mills had seen in his native Scotland the material progress the Acts of Union had brought to the Highlands since 1706. He could see no reason why the same improvements could not be made for the Indian peasants and urban artisans who were currently relentlessly ground down in poverty through overtaxation and at the same time denied basic human rights through the application of the rigid caste system. In his book he accused the Indian religious traditions of murdering bereaved wives and attacked those tyrannical emperors and princes who abused their position thereby growing fat on the back of the poor. The book went into four editions and was well received by the East India Company who began to put his radical ideas, especially those on legal reform, into practice.

There is a comprehensive account of the Scots' influence on British India in Arthur Herman's *The Scottish Enlightenment* (2002). Herman points out that 'a new British policy was already taking shape in India thanks to another coterie of Scots. They were the brilliant and dedicated protégées of Lord Minto, the Edinburgh educated governor general ... who oversaw the end of the East India Company's monopoly over British trade in 1813.'

In 1841, Charles Napier, whose father was born in Edinburgh and was tutored by David Hume, took over the governorship of Sind. He originally entered Sind with instructions to put down an insurrection but went on to exceed his orders by conquering the whole province. It was after doing so that he celebrated the victory with the now-famous pun by writing to his superiors, '*Peccavi*', the well-known Latin for 'I have sinned'. It was the most troublesome province of India, with frequent wars between the Hindu, Muslim and Sikh warriors. Napier was born to soldiering and joined the army when he was twelve. He fought under Wellington in Spain and was wounded numerous times before moving to India. His means of keeping order out in the empire was to administer 'a good thrashing first and great kindness afterward' which is how he tackled dissidents in Sind. He was, however, a political radical, a Chartist, with great sympathy for oppressed people everywhere and especially in India.

Herman makes the point that the sober truth is:

> many of the traditional regimes the British toppled both in India and elsewhere, had spent centuries making their subjects wretchedly unhappy. When their fate hung in the balance most of their populations refused to lift a finger to save them. For native peoples the British might not be their first choice but, in many case, thanks to Scots like Napier, they were better off than they had been.

Napier lowered taxes, established the port of Karachi, created a police force to keep order and banned the Hindu practice of suttee – that is burning a widow on her husband's funeral pyre. When the Brahmin priests protested that this was interfering with national custom, Napier replied, 'My nation also has a custom. When men burn women alive, we hang them. Let us all act according to national custom.'

On the death of Ranjit Singh there were difficulties of succession with both sons dying, one by poisoning and the other from masonry falling off an archway on return from his father's funeral. The British, finding the disturbances that followed intolerable, instigated the two Sikh Wars (1845–1846, 1848–1849), leading to the annexation of the Punjab. This direct action in Sind and Punjab provinces was prompted by the debacle in Afghanistan. British India was in a weakened position and since both these regions shared a border with Afghanistan, taking them over would strengthen Britain's hand in the Great Game.

The Raj system itself was ushered in under another Scottish governor general of India, General James Dalhousie (1812–1860). During his governorship the first railways were constructed, thousands of miles of telegraph wire were installed, and a national postal service created. Schools, roads and irrigation canals were all improved and expanded.

Dalhousie drastically changed social mores where women were concerned. He passed laws banning child marriage, polygamy and the killing of unwanted female children, and established, for the first time, schools for girls. In effect, he introduced more changes in seven years than had been enacted in centuries.

These reforms were not appreciated by everyone and some consider they were a contributing factor towards the Indian Mutiny of 1857. Exactly 100 years later, while studying empire in O level history, the 'mutiny' stimulated debate amongst my fellow fifth form historians at Cottesmore Secondary Modern School, Nottingham, as to whether it was a mutiny, a rebellion for independence, or a civil war. William Dalrymple in his meticulous research for his book *The Last Mughal* sums up the modern view that it was all of these things and more.

The death and destruction that ensued during the following months was finally brought to an end by two Scottish generals, the grizzled Glaswegian Colin Campbell, and Hugh Rose who became commander-in-chief of the British Army in India. The dual nature of the new British empire was now laid bare for all to see; on the one hand radical, humanitarian reforms but on the other, if challenged, the British did not hesitate to use force to maintain peace and order to keep India British.

The revolt had been crushed not only because of the determination of the British soldier but also because of the assistance of thousands of loyal Indians who fought alongside the British. Surprisingly, the warlike tribes, such as the Pathan and the Afghan in the north-west, remained neutral. As a result of the mutiny the East India Company was dissolved in 1858 and from then on India was under the direct rule of the British Government through a viceroy overseeing provincial governors assisted by a civil service of bureaucrats.

With the Indian Mutiny the Mughal rule of nearly 300 years came to an end as did the East India Company which had become a rapacious multinational whose bottom line was to please the shareholders. As has been shown, not all the servants of the company were into plundering India for ever more profit. However, the company won no favours when, in the process of putting down the mutiny, it inexcusably encouraged the looting and destruction of so much of the beauty of old Delhi. Its time had come, it had to go and was quickly replaced by a properly constituted colonial government in 1858.

All civil servants in India were subject to examination with Indian nationals, in theory, able to join. From now on Britain tightened its grip on all facets of Indian life, accelerating the reform process in all spheres – social, economic and political. Now with Indians receiving an education in English, India was transformed and regenerated. In particular, the health of the nation improved as did its infrastructure allowing long distances to be crossed in just a few hours by rail rather than many days, or even weeks, by horse and foot.

In 1864 Russia had taken Tashkent and it was obvious that it was only a matter of time before the Russians moved into the Pamir mountains.

It was estimated that during the previous century Russia had been expanding east and south into Asia at the rate of fifty-five miles a day. Similarly, the British empire since the Battle of Waterloo (1815) and the American Civil War (1865) had expanded by 100,000 square miles every year.

In anticipation of this clash of empires, which had all the hallmarks of being just as dramatic as the collision of continents, the British had already taken active steps to explore and survey the north-western fringe of India. It was becoming ever more imperative that the surveyors produced accurate maps showing the geography and settlement, not only out of intrinsic interest and commercial gain, but also with gathering importance to facilitate the movement of troops.

The German brothers, Adolph, Hermann and Robert Schlagintweit, from Munich, spent the years 1854–1857 in the service of the East India Company at the behest of their mentor, the geographer Alexander von Humboldt. Their main task was to carry out a magnetic survey during which they reached a height of 22,250 feet (6,780 metres) on Abi Gamin in the shadow of Kamet in the Kumaon Himal. This was a height record in 1855 but, not content with that, the following year Adolph marched up the Shigar Valley to become the first confirmed European to visit Askole, the last village before K2, five years before the next European visitor, Henry Haversham Godwin-Austen.

Adolph also reached the New Mustagh Pass at the head of the Chiring Glacier that flows into the Panmah Glacier. Sadly, Adolph, having made the dangerous crossing into Turkistan, was taken prisoner and beheaded as he was thought to be a Chinese spy. The three brothers had achieved more than most when exploring the region yet received scant acknowledgement by the authorities in India. Possibly this was not just the usual xenophobia but on account of the way the German brothers presented the results of their journeys. Their reports consisted of copious notes on their observations giving no clue to their personalities other than their attention to detail. The brothers would have received greater recognition had their reports been translated into English.

The main Survey of India was begun in 1802 with the 'Great Trigonometrical Survey' of the subcontinent. The backbone of the survey was the great arc of the meridian about 2,500 kilometres in extent from Cape Comorin at the southern tip of India to Dehra Dun in the north. This was completed in 1841 under the watchful eye of George Everest, the surveyor general from 1830–1843. His successor, Andrew Scott Waugh, pushed the survey into the foothills including Kashmir during the years 1855–1864.

Thomas George Montgomerie (1830–1878) was put in charge of this survey along with his able assistants William Johnson, who was born in India,

Captain Thomas George Montgomerie, R.E.

and Henry Haversham Godwin-Austen. Montgomerie came from Ayrshire where his father was Provost of Irvine and colonel in the Ayrshire Yeomanry. At the age of fifteen young Thomas entered the East India Company's military academy at Addiscombe in Surrey. He went out to India in 1851 where he spent his first tour of duty with the Bengal Engineers working on the Hindustan–Tibet road before joining the Great Trigonometrical Survey under Waugh. For the next ten years he led the way in surveying an area of 70,000 square miles of Jammu and Kashmir.

Kenneth Mason, a former superintendent of the Survey of India, wrote, in his classic history of Himalayan exploration, *Abode of Snow* (1955), that 'Montgomerie, an engineer officer, was the brain and organiser behind the whole survey of Kashmir.' He planned the network of stations that covered the mountains and did much of the preliminary reconnaissance. He was helped in this by retaining very friendly relations with Gulab Singh, the maharaja and later his son, Ranbir Singh. It was early on in the survey in September 1856 that Montgomerie made his now-famous sketch of the two most prominent peaks in the Karakoram range while he was taking measurements of the surrounding mountains from a survey station on Harmukh Peak (16,870 feet/5,143 metres), just north of Srinagar and the Vale of Kashmir.

It was a lucky break in the clouds that enabled him to suddenly see the Karakoram range 130 miles away to the north-east. The two prominent peaks he labelled K1 and K2, noting in his survey log that K2 seemed the higher. He and his subordinate surveyors eventually labelled thirty-two peaks with a K, to remain so until local names could be found for them. In 1906 Sir Sidney Burrard reminded explorers and geographers that the policy of the Survey of India and the Royal Geographical Society was 'the nomenclature of a mountain region should not be forced: it should grow spontaneously, and we should never invent a name until its absence has become inconvenient.'

K1 became known by its local name, Masherbrum, but K2, so remote that no local name had been attributed to it, remained K2. There was hardly any change in the first recorded height. In 1858 it was computed by George Shelverton from stations in Kashmir to be 28,287 feet, or 8,621 metres, and therefore the second highest peak in the world. Currently the accepted height is 8,611 metres (28,251 feet), a difference of only ten metres, which is a strong indication of just how thorough and accurate the servants of the Survey of India were. K3 was eventually renamed Broad Peak, K4 Gasherbrum II, K5 Gasherbrum I and K6 was first named Bride Peak by Conway but then renamed Chogolisa. This is the mountain where the great Hermann Buhl lost his life after making the first ascent of Broad Peak in 1957. Despite the upheaval caused by the Indian Mutiny it was decided to continue the survey, if only to impress upon the local maharajahs and their subjects that the British were optimistic there would be a speedy end to hostilities.

Montgomerie, more than any of the senior surveyors, trained local hill men to carry on the survey of the north of India and beyond, where the British surveyors were forbidden to travel. They were specially chosen for their fitness, intelligence and loyalty. They were known as the pundits and bravely went about their business disguised as pilgrims visiting holy sites, knowing that if they were discovered to be in the pay of the British they risked a nasty end. They were shown all manner of ingenious ways to record data as they travelled, all of which helped the British to construct maps and fill in more of the blank spaces in such areas as Chitral, Chilas, Gilgit and Swat in the Karakoram, and further afield into Tibet where pundit 'AK' made the first circuit of Everest (see *Spying for the Raj*, 2006, by Jules Stewart).

6 **The Blanks on the Map**

The first Westerner into the environs of the Ogre was Henry Haversham Godwin-Austen (1834–1923) when he and his colleagues carried the Survey of India deep into the Karakoram mountains. By the mid-nineteenth century the British had fully realised the importance of the Karakoram as a natural boundary between British India and the fabled lands beyond in Central Asia. Godwin-Austen was expected to unravel the topography of the area and put it on the map. He was born near Newton Abbot, Devon, and educated at the Royal Grammar School, Guildford, before joining the army where he was taught military surveying at the Royal Military College at Sandhurst. Catherine Moorehead has written the definitive story of Godwin-Austen in her book *The K2 Man (and his Molluscs)*.

Godwin-Austen's work brought him eventually into Baltistan where he became the first confirmed Westerner to see the Hispar, Biafo, Panmah and Baltoro glaciers. In 1862 he produced a reconnaissance map on a scale of a quarter inch to the mile covering an incredible 3,700 square miles of some of the most rugged landscapes in the world. To unravel the topography of such a vast mountain area was a magnificent achievement, made possible by Godwin-Austen's phenomenal fitness and drive to see around the next corner, and by his hardworking and loyal Indian assistants.

Between 7 July and 28 September 1861 he ascended several peaks in the vicinity of Skardu including Marshakala, 16,919 feet (5,157 metres), some twelve kilometres due north of Skardu, when he most likely fixed the height of the Ogre at 23,914 feet (7,285 metres), which was then designated '18/43m' by the Indian Survey of 1855–1860.

He was well suited for surveying work out in the field, being physically strong, wiry and endowed with boundless energy. He was not a technical climber but he was a fine mountaineer having a natural affinity with rugged landscape. Mason, who went on to be one of the founder members of the Himalayan Club, wrote in *Abode of Snow* that Godwin-Austen was probably the greatest mountaineer of his day.

K2 viewed from the flanks of Broad Peak.

His name became forever associated with K2. Montgomerie requested Godwin-Austen should not only map the Mustagh Pass and the Baltoro Glacier but should determine whether or not K2 was situated on the main Karakoram watershed, and if it therefore lay within the British empire. From observations made above the pasture of Urdukas, high up on an outlying spur of Masherbrum, Godwin-Austen was able to show that K2 was on the main divide. He thus became the first European to see K2 close up. Montgomerie had suggested Godwin-Austen's name should be substituted for the appellation K2. Godwin-Austen himself was against this relabelling and the idea was dropped. He was, however, immortalised by having the glacier that curves around the east side of K2 named after him.

In the late summer of 1861, during his explorations, Godwin-Austen had marched up the true right bank of the Biafo Glacier for five miles; he then ascended a 'low knob' of 12,645 feet (3,854 metres) from where he could see Latok and Baintha Brakk. He also explored the Panmah Glacier and the lower end of the Choktoi Glacier. During these investigations he must have had excellent views of the Latok mountains and the Ogre.

Godwin-Austen completed this remarkable season by marching up to the herding hamlet of Arandu from where he carried out an original exploration of the Kero Lungma Glacier. On 4 September he and his party, after cutting steps in steep snow, reached Nushik La (16,370 feet/4,990 metres). It is

Henry Haversham Godwin-Austen.

called the Uyum Haghuch Pass on the 1939 Shipton map. Most people will prefer Nushik La, from where Godwin-Austen could see twelve miles of the Hispar Glacier and remarked, 'No glacier in the whole of the Himalayas can exceed this in magnitude of all its features'; apart from the Siachen, which is the longest subpolar glacier, he was correct. He retreated after noting how steep the descent would be, satisfied that it would be of no military significance. This is a reminder that one of the main reasons behind this survey of the North-West Frontier was for military intelligence, so that troops could be despatched more efficiently.

William Johnson, who was born in India to English parents, was another exceptionally energetic surveyor working in Kashmir and the Karakoram from 1857 to 1865. Mason in *Abode of Snow* reports on his work: 'In 1861 two of his stations were above 20,000 feet: in 1862 seven. For six years, four of his stations were the highest triangulation stations in the world.' He later somewhat blotted his copybook by travelling over the Karakoram Pass into Chinese Turkistan to stay with a rebel ruler in Khotan without permission of the Government of India. He also claimed he had climbed E61, a mountain in the Kunlun range of 23,890 feet (7,281 metres). The Survey of India on checking Johnson's figures discounted this claim but not before it was taken up by leading climbers of the day including Douglas Freshfield, Norman Collie and Godwin-Austen 'who did not know all the facts' according to Mason.

It is perhaps timely to point out that just as very few peaks in the Himalaya, if any, could be climbed without the help of local porters transporting food, fuel and equipment to the base of the mountains, there would have been no mapping at that time without the help of native porter, known as khalasis, carrying heavy and awkward loads of survey poles and theodolites over very rough terrain to the summits of peaks and points at rarefied heights.

There were around twenty battles fought between the Indian Army and local tribesmen in the North-West Frontier area between 1863 and 1901. In 1889 the Gilgit Agency was established, partly to ensure the local area was not infiltrated by Russians and also to help keep the peace between the various tribes. The constant fighting between the Hunza and Nagar tribesmen was only brought to an end when both sides were defeated by soldiers of the Raj in 1891. Further exploration could now take place with calm restored to the area.

Francis Younghusband (1863–1942) appeared on the scene in 1887 when, at the age of twenty-four, he travelled mostly on horseback, overland from Peking across the Gobi Desert and over the Old Mustagh Pass back into British India. The 4,000-mile journey from Peking to Rawalpindi took seven months. He was born in the foothills of the Himalaya at Murree into a British military family. His uncle, Robert Shaw, was a well-known explorer of Central Asia and became young Francis' hero. He was groomed for great and solitary adventures in that, like so many of the explorers and pioneer mountaineers of the time, he was sent back from India as an infant to be looked after by strict relatives during his formative years. In his case the aunts were quite brutal – loneliness would have been something he would have had to come to terms with – and that would equip him well for the rest of his life when spending months in isolation. He was enrolled at Clifton College, Bristol, then entered Sandhurst in 1881 to be commissioned a subaltern in the King's Dragoon Guards.

Out in India he managed to inveigle a period of leave up in Manchuria. He was asked to check out the porous Chinese frontier for evidence of Russian penetration. Rather than return from Peking by sea he decided to travel overland. Near the end of his incredible journey he received a letter at Kashgar from Colonel Mark Bell, head of Indian intelligence, suggesting that Younghusband should 'strike out a new line and explore the route to India by way of the Mustagh Pass leading into Baltistan and then Kashmir'. Bell, who had just missed meeting Younghusband, would himself be taking the more frequently travelled Karakoram Pass.

Younghusband was, he wrote later, 'thrilled with such exploration' to cross the main Karakoram divide right by the second highest peak in the world and the chance to emulate his uncle. Robert Shaw was actually the first

Concordia as seen from K2, with Bride Peak (later renamed Chogolisa) on the left.

Westerner into Kashgar, closely followed by George Hayward in 1868. Sadly, Hayward, during a solo journey to Dardistan, had his head chopped off at Darkot in 1870 and Robert Shaw, when only thirty-nine, died of rheumatic fever in Mandalay in 1879.

Younghusband made plans for the journey in Yarkand, gathering together a guide, ponies, porters and all his supplies. His chief guide was from Askole, named Wali, and was the last man known to have crossed the Mustagh Pass twenty-five years before. The caravan broke new ground discovering and crossing the Aghil Mountains, the Shaksgam River, a major tributary of the Yarkand, and finally the Sarpo Laggo Glacier. This was the first European sighting of a glacier flowing down the northern flanks of the Karakoram. It was here Younghusband beheld K2, 'a peak of almost perfect proportion, clothed in a glittering mantle of pure white snow and ice … standing head and shoulders above all the other mountains.' This was also the first time a European had seen the north side of K2.

Mountaineering was a new experience for Younghusband who had never previously been on a glacier but was now to spend three days on the snow and ice en route to the 'old' Mustagh Pass. It took Wali some time to locate the least difficult way over. They had attempted to cross one pass unsuccessfully which they named the 'new' Mustagh Pass.

The plan was for Younghusband, Wali and four Balti men to depart for the pass leaving Liu-San and the rest of the men in charge of the ponies. They reached the summit of the pass after a six-hour plod through deep snow, breathless but otherwise in good spirits, until they looked over the pass at a precipice of ice and rock. With success in sight they overcame their fears and inexperience and began the descent. Wali hacked away at the ice with a pickaxe producing large steps to accommodate the native footwear which was little more than a leather sock. They became wet, soggy and very slippery on the bare ice, so to obtain more friction Younghusband hit upon the idea of tying handkerchiefs around each instep.

They also made use of baggage ropes, turbans and even their cummerbunds all tied together and, as it turned out, these were strong enough to withstand a Balti tumbling down the ice. By going from one rock island poking up out of the ice cliffs to another, they eventually reached level ground and the Baltoro Glacier. In three days they were in Askole but he wasn't impressed: 'That was a dirty little village, the trees and the fields looked fresh and green, but the houses and inhabitants were repulsively dirty; and the latter by no means well disposed.' But they did provide food, 'greasy and dirty though it was – mutton stew, rice and tea – down it went. More and more of it until I thought I could never fill myself.'

They found the villagers none too friendly and, surprisingly, unfriendly to Wali who had, after all, been away a long time. The reason was they saw Wali as a traitor who had now reopened a door to strangers from the north, a door they all thought was well and truly shut. They had thought themselves safe from being overwhelmed in their beds by Hunza men. Wali had now given the village cause to be fearful and he in turn found his own life threatened. He would not leave Younghusband's side and left the village with him for protection.

Before they left, however, they managed to persuade the Askole men to take supplies over the newly opened Mustagh Pass to the awaiting Liu-San so that he and the pony men could reach Leh via the Karakoram Pass well to the east. Amazingly, Younghusband, having recovered from all the greasy food eaten in such quantities, still had energy left for a reconnaissance via the Panmah Glacier to the other side of the 'new' (western) Mustagh Pass. The Chiring Glacier, tumbling down from the pass in a maze of séracs, obviously offered no easy route over from India to Central Asia. Younghusband had now carried out his reconnaissance to the letter and indeed had found there was no feasible trade or military route over the watershed by either the old or the new Mustagh passes.

He walked out through Skardu and Leh to Simla where he eventually met his servant, Liu-San, who had, over six weeks, walked around with the ponies.

Sir Francis Younghusband.

Liu-San was suffering from pleurisy for which Younghusband treated him and sent him back to China by sea. Liu-San had been with Younghusband from Beijing on the whole of the 4,000-mile journey, but his appreciation of his servant was perhaps typically qualified:

> He was a Chinaman, and therefore not a perfect animal, but he understood his business thoroughly, and he did it. So for a journey across the entire breadth of the Chinese Empire I could scarcely have found a better man. As long as he felt that he was 'running' me, and that it was his business to convey me, like a bundle of goods, from one side of China to the other, he worked untiringly. And the success of the journey is in no small degree due to this single servant, who had not feared to accompany me throughout.

Younghusband's journeys were ultimately under the auspices of the Government of India, more for political reasons than exploration. However, it only takes the reading of a few chapters of Younghusband's many books to realise he would never be satisfied with regimental duties focusing on the parade ground and officers' mess. He had tasted the call of the wild and needed

Wali leading the way over the Mustagh Pass, hacking at the ice with a pickaxe bought in Yarkand.

to follow his yearnings to be off looking beyond the next horizon. There was another thread to Younghusband's character and that was his conviction that there was more to life than outward appearances. So there was not only his need to explore the planet, but also he had a strong inner quest of self-discovery. This was to characterise him as being introspective, romantic and something of a mystic.

He did, as a consequence of his outward quest, provide more information of the geography of the region. The area of unknown mountains was shrinking year by year as the political climate became more conducive to travel and exploration. Younghusband returned to the north side of the Karakoram in 1889. He had been given the task of locating secret passes by which raiders from Hunza were attacking caravans of merchandise travelling between Leh and Yarkand.

Sir Mortimer Durand, the foreign secretary to the Government of India, had personally tasked Younghusband to find out all he could of the rumours that the Emir of Hunza was in talks with the Russian emissary, the formid-able Pole, Captain Bronislav Grombchevsky (1855–1926), who was in the pay of the Imperial Russian Army. The British were now seriously worried with the Russians having extended a railway line right across Central Asia past Samarkand. To the British in India it seemed a strong possibility that a Russian army could quickly mount an invasion. With six Gurkhas Young-husband checked out various passes and put the Saltoro and Shimshal passes on the map.

He also met Grombchevsky, who was accompanied by a small party of Cossacks, when they were exploring the Raskam Valley for their respective governments in 1889. They were in identical positions and, in fact, are now seen to have been two of the great rivals of the Great Game. At the time they quickly understood the situation, being two of a kind who had separately identified the area where they met as being important. They both knew that the Great Game was approaching the End Game. If Younghusband had any reservations about the Russians before the meeting he had none afterwards: Grombchevsky informed him that Russian soldiers only had one thought and that was to invade India.

Despite being on opposite sides of the fence they respected each other and parted as friends. That was one of the few times the players of the Great Game met head to head at the frontier of their respective empires. By 1890 Younghusband had been transferred to the Indian Political Service. From then on he served as a political officer, on secondment from the British Army. He later led the military 'mission' into Tibet. After slaughtering with Maxim guns several hundred Tibetans who were armed only with swords and flint-locks, he had a powerful religious experience on a hilltop outside Lhasa and spent a large part of his remaining life working for the interfaith movement.

Not until the people of Hunza and those of Nagar were pacified was there any realistic expectation of organising private expeditions into the mountains in the region of the Hispar and Biafo glaciers. There had been almost constant conflict between these two adjacent areas and, even today, there is a degree of tension between the two who share the same country but quite a different version of their religion.

7   **Early Mountaineering**

By 1892 everything was in place for a thorough exploration of the Hispar, Biafo and Baltoro glaciers. All three had been discovered with the major peaks plotted and measured. The semi-autonomous tribes of the area, who had previously spent most of their time – besides tending their fields and pastures – raiding each other's villages and ambushing passing trade, and killing merchants and absconding with their merchandise, had now been brought to heel and pacified by the army of the Raj.

Further afield there had been other developments favourable to travelling out to this last frontier of empire. With the opening of the Suez Canal in 1869 and the increasing network of railway lines in the Indus valley, not to mention the installation of thousands of miles of telegraph wire, journey times were forever decreasing. Martin Conway decided to launch the first private multi-disciplinary mountaineering expedition to the Himalaya in 1892. There had been other incursions into the Himalaya by private individuals – naturalists, geologists, and hunters of birds and beasts – and also in 1883 the barrister William Graham, with Swiss guides, had visited the Himalaya with no other intention it seems than to enjoy climbing high. Having been inspired by Whymper's expedition to the Andes in 1880, Conway decided to include artists, naturalists and surveyors – as well as climbers – in his expedition.

Once the European Alps had been thoroughly explored and mapped then those mountaineers who revelled in mountain exploration had to look to the Greater Ranges. Similarly, with all the mountains of the Alps now climbed and with all their prominent features successfully tackled by many routes, pioneers longing to climb elegant lines and challenging unclimbed features had to go to the Himalaya. To pioneer new routes was the main reason for me, and for friends of mine, to travel out to the Himalaya, just as it was back in 1892 for Conway. Having explored the Alps from end to end, he now set himself the task of exploring 'the heart of the Karakoram'.

Conway was born in Rochester in 1856, the son of the rector of St Margaret's Church in Westminster. He was educated at Repton and Trinity

Martin Conway (1856–1937). Reproduced by kind permission
of the Alpine Club Photo Library, London.

College, Cambridge. He became well known as an art critic of early Flemish
artists and was later Professor of Art at University College, Liverpool. By the
time he had left Cambridge he had several Alpine seasons behind him and
in 1877 he was elected a member of the Alpine Club. Conway was like many
other club members of the time, such as Douglas Freshfield, good on snow
and ice but tended to avoid rock climbing. He was proud of his interest in
mountain exploration, declaring his credentials in the *Alpine Journal* of 1891
where he divided mountaineers into 'centrists and excentrists', according to
whether they based themselves at one popular centre of climbing, or ranged
free throughout the Alps, crossing over peaks and passes from one valley
to the next.

Conway's view of the ideal mountain climber was one who:

> loves first and foremost to wander far and wide among the moun-
> tains, does not sleep willingly two consecutive nights in the same
> inn, hates centres, gets tired of a district, always wants to see what
> is on the other side of any range of hills, prefers passes to peaks but
> hates not getting to the top of anything he starts for, chooses the
> easiest and most normal route, likes to know the names of all
> the peaks in view, and cannot bear to see a group of peaks none
> of which he has climbed.

Needless to say his ideal mountaineer bore a close resemblance to himself. By temperament Conway was ideally suited to organising and leading the disparate group of individuals he was putting together for his expedition. In *A Century of Mountaineering* Arnold Lunn gives an excellent portrayal of Conway's character. Conway tended towards showing patience with everyone as far as possible neither making enemies or close friends with anyone, although it is said you cannot have one without the other. There was an exception to this rule and that was Oscar Eckenstein, a member of the expedition who was sacked before the end.

Lunn, in reference to a time later in life when Conway became a politician, notes that:

> Forlorn hopes and lost causes might stir his sympathy but could never engage his active support. He cherished a mild but friendly disdain for the human race, but the stupidities of mankind were never allowed to disturb his tranquillity. Montaigne remarked that it was taking a man's opinions too seriously to burn him alive for them. Conway, who had so much in common with Montaigne, might have added that it was taking a man's stupidities too seriously to burn with indignation because of them.

Despite his wife's misgivings Conway decided to occupy his time by putting together this Karakoram expedition. In fact, Conway applied to his wife's American stepfather Manton Marble for sponsorship. He finally agreed to this provided Conway was able to secure the support of both *The Times* newspaper and the Royal Geographical Society (RGS) so that he could achieve a higher profile to help increase audience numbers at his lectures and also sales of his books. He was a keen bibliophile but also wrote books himself on art appreciation.

Conway did eventually receive RGS support; the society had since 1830 sponsored and indirectly publicised expeditions mainly to Africa and the Arctic. Exploration to Asia was recognised when in 1865 Montgomerie received the RGS Founder's Medal 'for his great trigonometrical journey from the plains of the Punjab to the Karakoram range'.

The only actual explorer to the Himalaya during the Great Game to be financially supported by the RGS was George Hayward, who was given £300 and loaned surveying equipment in 1868 to explore the Pamir mountains. The RGS was strictly non-political and yet the president at the time, Sir Henry Rawlinson, known to be a Russophobe, requested Hayward to map as much of the Pamirs as he could as they were directly in the path of Russian expansion towards India. Hayward was awarded a Gold Medal by the RGS, but lost their support over a matter of principle and, as mentioned previously, he was beheaded in Darkot in 1870.

The ultimate accolade for many young explorers was an invitation to lecture at the RGS. This is what Francis Younghusband did in 1888, speaking about his travels across Asia and through the Mustagh Pass. In that same year he became the youngest fellow of the RGS and two years later received the Founder's Medal. In 1919 he became president of the RGS, an appointment of considerable significance to launching the early expeditions to Mount Everest of which Younghusband was a great supporter.

The council of the RGS took some persuading to support Conway's proposed expedition to the Karakoram and only offered a provisional grant of £200 dependent upon scientific results. Similarly Kew Gardens promised a grant only if he came back with an interesting collection of plants. This was encouragement enough so he set about putting his team together. Albert Mummery was on his list despite the fact he had opposite views to Conway of what climbing was all about. To Mummery, 'The essence of the sport lies not in ascending a peak but in struggling with and overcoming difficulties'. Mummery was a brilliant mountaineer and accomplished rock climber with such routes as the Zmutt Ridge on the Matterhorn under his belt. After spending time with Conway in the Alps, Mummery came to realise their essential differences and that Conway was unlikely to attempt K2 or any other major summit so he turned the offer down.

Conway then approached another fine mountaineer, Oscar Eckenstein, born in Britain of an English mother and a German father. Like his father he had strong leanings towards socialism and was also an outspoken critic of the empire and the Alpine Club, which begs the question as to why Conway invited him aboard his expedition. Apart from his climbing abilities he also had a mathematical and engineering bent, in fact over time he has remained best known for inventing the ten-point crampon. Eckenstein looked forward to climbing peaks and Conway had designs on Eckenstein contributing to the scientific side of the expedition; neither aim was fulfilled.

Matthias Zurbriggen, a Swiss-Italian guide well known to Conway and especially Eckenstein, became the mainstay of the expedition, being the most experienced mountaineer and utterly dependable. The expedition artist was Arthur McCormick, an unknown watercolourist with no mountaineering experience but who had a wealthy sponsor to pay his expenses.

They were all to meet another key member of the expedition, Charles Granville Bruce of the 5th Gurkha Rifles, in Abbottabad. Bruce was a very strong and experienced mountaineer who had taken part in several skirmishes during the 'pacification' of the North-West Frontier provinces. He went on to lead two of the early Everest expeditions. Bruce would be providing four Gurkhas from this frontier force, Karbir Thapa, Parbir Thapa, Harkbir Thapa and Amar Singh, who would remain with the expedition throughout. There were several aspects to this expedition which made it a first of the genre, setting a pattern for all future large exploratory mountaineering expeditions to this day, in particular the hiring of strong local hill men to carry heavy loads up into the thin cold air. With the advent of such expeditions in the central Himalaya and especially in Sikkim and Nepal, expeditions became more likely to hire Sherpas.

The English party, with Parbir Thapa, left Fenchurch Street station for the Albert Dock on 5 February 1892. Five weeks later on 7 March they arrived, via the Suez Canal, at Karachi. That same evening they took the train which during the next four days brought them to within a few miles of Abbottabad. It was there they met up with Bruce and his Gurkhas and became Bruce's guests for two weeks until their baggage caught up with them. They went by *ekka,* a very uncomfortable horse-drawn two-wheeled carriage without springs, to Srinagar in the Vale of Kashmir.

Just as Darjeeling, Kathmandu, Dehra Dun and Manali became the centres of operations for mountaineering in the Himalaya, Srinagar was the town where mountaineers gathered and collected supplies before heading off into the Karakoram. After the partition of India in 1947 Srinagar became less important in this regard as most expeditions made Rawalpindi and Skardu their starting point.

By early June, Conway was ready to move north to Gilgit and the Hunza valley, one of the most beautiful of all valleys. It is surrounded by magnificent mountains which are not obscured by forested lower hills but are right there, revealed. For example, Rakaposhi has a dazzling snow and ice face that plunges over 5,000 metres from the 7,788-metre summit down to the valley at only 2,400 metres. The only comparable vertical interval is that of the Rupal Face of Nanga Parbat. The climbing of Rakaposhi had been one of Conway's objectives but was abandoned after the expedition watched avalanches pour down its north face.

After exploring the area of Bagrot and the Hunza valley they made their way on 10 June, towards Nagar and the Hispar Glacier. They were the first tourists to be taken round the fort at Nilt which was stormed and captured only six months before in December 1891. It had been a fierce battle during which Colonel Durand in charge of the British troops was wounded and Captain Manners Smith with his party of Indian troops, including Harkbir, bravely stormed the defences and decided the campaign. Manners Smith was awarded the Victoria Cross for his gallantry. Harkbir gave Conway and the members a full account of the action and his part in it. From then on the area remained far more peaceful and trade increased without the threat of

View to the east from the top of Hispar Pass with the Ogre seen by Europeans and drawn for the first time.

caravans of merchandise being plundered by bandits.

Early in July they reached the Hispar Glacier and on 3 July Bruce, Eckenstein, Amar Singh and Karbir went over the Nushik La to Arandu for more supplies. It was from this village that Godwin-Austen had reached the pass nearly twenty years earlier. By 18 July the expedition was all together when they made the first European crossing of the Hispar Pass.

On reaching the pass, Conway and his party were transfixed by the expanse of snow and shapely mountains all around. He wrote in the expedition book: 'Before us lay a basin or lake of snow... From the midst of the snowy lake rose a series of mountain islands, white like the snow that buried their bases and there were endless bays and straits as of white water nestling amongst them.'

Later, as they descended from the Hispar La towards the Biafo Glacier, Conway refers to their next camp on the expanse of snow as Snow Lake Camp. He is disappointed that because of porter illness they do not have two or three days to explore Snow Lake. His last reference was when 'We had finally left the open lake behind and entered the broad corridor of the Biafo Glacier.' Shipton in his *Blank on the Map* (1938) wonders how much importance Conway intended to be attached to the name Snow Lake. The implication is not that much.

Was this naming the great expanse of snow as Snow Lake simply a reflection of Conway's artistic temperament and a spontaneous subjective analogy, rather than an objectively considered geographical fact? In short it resembled a lake without being a lake, not necessarily a landlocked lake of snow and no mention or intention to suggest it was some subpolar ice cap as others did later. It is most probable he saw the snow as a lake in the same way as mountaineers, when looking down on to an inversion of cloud down in the valley, refer to it as a sea of cloud – and not just mountaineers but also poets. Wordsworth in his *Prelude* wrote about an experience of a cloud inversion on Snowdon:

... and on the shore
I found myself of a huge sea of mist,
Which, meek and silent, rested at my feet.
A hundred hills their dusky backs upheaved
All over this still ocean; and beyond,
Far, far beyond, the vapours shot themselves,
In headlands, tongues and promontory shapes,
Into the sea, the real sea ...

In an article in the *Geographical Journal* of 1892 Conway refers to 'A seemingly flat area of snow ... there was no visible outlet to this lake but there was the suggestion of the existence of one round the corner to the right, hidden by a near snowy ridge.' This was the Biafo Glacier by which they travelled down to Askole passing the Ogre en route – the same glacier that over the last 10,000 years or more has helped shape the mountains that contain it, including the Ogre and all the Latok peaks.

Conway gives no reason why he called point 23914 'the Ogre' – it could have been on account of its appearance. We may never know why he called it the Ogre but it seems most likely that it was him that did give the mountain this name, as on the map of 1875 reproduced in *The Apricot Road to Yarkand* by Salman Rashid, point 23914 is unnamed. He writes that he first caught sight of the Ogre two days before crossing the Hispar Pass – but how did he know that? Was it on an early Survey of India map of the region that he had with him? Certainly he makes no mention of gleaning local information about the peak. In shape it is no way as inspiring as the Matterhorn or Shivling, it is rather large and squat in appearance, made up of buttresses and pillars of granite, interspersed with ribs of ice and snow, leading up to a three-headed summit. With a bit of imagination it could give the impression of being not unlike a giant, warty ogre.

One of the many achievements of this expedition was the surveying, but unfortunately the weather was not always kind. Some confusion set in when Conway having referred to the Ogre as seen from the Hispar Pass, then referred to quite a different Ogre when proceeding down the Biafo Glacier. From the pass Conway wrote, 'Before us lay a basin or lake of snow. This lake was bounded to the north and east by white ridges, and to the south by the splendid row of needle-peaks, the highest of which, the Ogre, had looked at us over the pass two days before.' This prose is accompanied by a sketch entitled 'View to the east from top of the Hispar Pass' on which the Ogre is recognisable from modern-day photographs and Shipton's map. On Conway's map he marked point 23914 in approximately the same position as on Shipton's map, but for some reason does not name it the Ogre.

This watercolour appears in Conway's book labelled as 'The Ogre from Ogre Camp'. It is so obviously not the Ogre he referred to looking east from the Hispar Pass. It may always remain a mystery as to why Conway caused this confusion to arise. Amongst climbers the peak as illustrated is now referred to as Conway's Ogre and appears on the Shipton map as Uzun Brakk.

Shipton had abandoned the name Ogre in favour of a local name, Baintha Brakk, and fixed the height at 23,900 feet.

The name probably derives from the fact that *baintha* means a pasture and *brakk* a rocky summit. There is a pasture called Baintha by the Biafo Glacier at the entrance to the Baintha Lukpar Glacier so logically Baintha Brakk could be interpreted as the rocky peak above the pasture. Muhammad Iqbal, the son of Haji Mehdi from Askole, has informed me that Baintha is the place of pasture of the Askole village, and Nazir Sabir, who has contacted various Balti, reports that the name Baintha Brakk was in use a long time before any foreigners visited the region. It should be noted that Pakistani travel writer Salman Rashid has found 'that *Baintha* probably derives either from *bainthak*, the Balti for chough or from Urdu *baithak* a seat, throne, resting or meeting place'. If it is the latter then it would tie in with the interpretation that it is the 'rocky peak above the pasture'. Catherine Moorehead has collaborated with me on the naming and positioning of the Ogre/Baintha Brakk.

As Conway and his team proceeded down the Biafo Glacier from Snow Lake on 19 July 1892 they found themselves passing a series of spires and needles not unlike the Chamonix Aiguilles:

> but these needles outjut them in steepness, outnumber them in multitude, and outreach them in size. The highest of them flings its royal summit more than 23,000 feet into the air, and looks abroad over a field of mountains that finds no superior in the world. I named the ridge on the north the Ogre's Fingers, and the great peak the Ogre.

In his book there is a watercolour (reproduced in black and white) titled 'Ogre's Fingers from Ogre's Camp' and on it the aiguille to the left is recognisable as Conway's Ogre and the broad peak at the back as possibly the upper part of the Ogre, but of course this was not pointed out in the title of the watercolour. On the next page is another watercolour, again in monochrome, entitled 'The Ogre from Ogre's Camp', but what is depicted is 'The Ogre's Fingers', the main one now known in general parlance amongst climbers as Conway's Ogre and officially on maps as Uzun Brakk after the glacier below it on the north side. Could it be the confusion arose simply because of an error made by the publishers, or by Conway himself, when labelling the illustrations? The expedition descended to Askole to regroup before doubling back up the Baldu to explore the Baltoro Glacier and K2.

It is interesting to know that Conway understood that he was the first to reach the point where all the glaciers came together and to which he gave

The magnificent north side of the Ogre, first seen by Martin Conway and his team from the Hispar Pass in 1892. This photograph was taken by Nobuo Kuwahara from a camp on South Tahu Ratum Glacier in 1975.

the name Place de la Concorde, today known as Concordia. It is now an accepted fact that the little-known, publicity-shy Italian Robert Lerco was in the area two years before. He may well have climbed some way up the south east spur of K2, now known as the Abruzzi Spur and the way K2 was first climbed.

Place de la Concorde is surrounded by an amphitheatre of mountains unsurpassed in number, height and grandeur. They include K2, Gasherbrum IV – the 'Shining Mountain', and the sublime Bride Peak, Chogolisa. Conway was in ecstasy proclaiming:

> Here, indeed, was a highway into another world with which man had nothing to do. It might lead into a land of dragons, or giants, or ghosts. The very thought of man vanished in such surroundings, and there was no sign of animal life. The view was like seen music.

Conway was desperate to climb high and after climbing Crystal Peak to over 6,000 metres (19,685 feet) he identified the mountain he was looking for, 'The most brilliant of all the mountains we saw'. He named it Golden Throne, which is now called Baltoro Kangri (7,312 metres/23,990 feet). He and his team climbed in 'Mr Eckenstein's claws' up a ridge on the mountain to where there was an impassable gap, so that is where they had to stop their ascent. They named the point Pioneer Peak, then thought to be 7,010 metres (23,000 feet); subsequent measurement has shown it to be 6,499 metres (21,320 feet). At the time he claimed to have got higher than anyone else, but that would be discounting the claims made by William Graham to have climbed Kabru (7,394 metres/24,260 feet) in 1883.

Oscar Eckenstein was frustrated that so little time had been allowed for ascending peaks. He was very different in character and background to Conway, and, being outspoken, clashed with him. He was also suffering gastric troubles and left the expedition. Conway was complimented by his guide Zurbriggen, who said, 'I had to work all day and I lost my temper. My Herr worked all day, and all night too, and never lost his temper.' It seems Conway lived up to his reputation to remain in a state of equanimity, at least to all outward appearances.

In 1902 Eckenstein led a mainly British expedition to K2 but found himself under arrest by the deputy commissioner of Rawalpindi. It took him three weeks to extricate himself and rejoin the expedition. Eckenstein had no idea why he had been prevented from entering Kashmir, but it was the opinion of one of his notorious team members, Aleister Crowley, that the delay was due to Conway's intervention. Crowley's opinion counted for nothing at the time since he was known as the 'Great Beast 666' and was involved in drugs, sex and black magic. However, another member, the distinguished Guy Knowles who had largely funded the expedition and had been threatened by Crowley with a revolver, nevertheless also felt that Conway, who at the time was Alpine Club president, had 'Interposed to put obstacles in Eckenstein's way', and the authorities, 'did not relent till faced with a threat to expose the whole story to the *Daily Telegraph*'. The truth may never be known whether it was Conway's spite, or government suspicion that Eckenstein was a spy with his Prussian-Jewish-sounding name, that had the leader of the first expedition to K2 locked up and barred for the first three weeks of the expedition.

Despite dissension Conway's expedition added considerable cartographic detail to Godwin-Austen's work by increasing the area of reconnaissance mapping to 5,000 square miles. In the *Alpine Journal* of August 1893 there is an account of 'Climbing in the Karakorams' by Conway accompanied by a very detailed map on a scale of 1:400,000 showing the expedition's

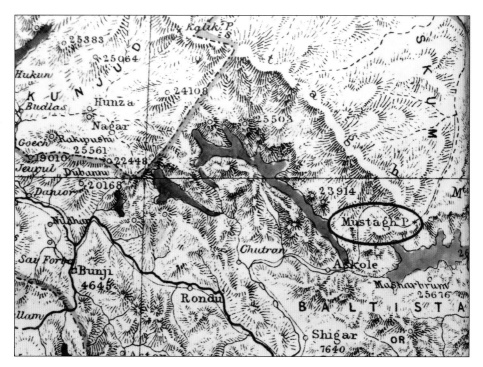

I am grateful to Salman Rashid for making this map available from his book, *The Apricot Road to Yarkand*. The legend with the map indicates 'Mapped on the basis of the Surveys made by British and Russian Officers up to 1875. Compiled under the orders of Colonel J.C. Walker ... Superintendent Great Trigonometrical Survey of India ... Dehra Doon, June 1875.' Point 23,914 is the Ogre. The Biafo Glacier is to the west of the Ogre.

journeys up the Hispar and down the Biafo glaciers before going up on to the Baltoro Glacier. The Royal Geographical Society later published in two sheets maps on a scale of one inch to two miles that were invaluable to future explorers entering the region.

Conway generously acknowledged his debt to his predecessors, especially Godwin-Austen, in letters and articles published in the *Alpine Journal* and the *Geographical Journal*. It was most likely Godwin-Austen first fixed point 23900/23914 from survey stations around Skardu in the early 1860s. Conway had broken new territory, on the ground, and in the conduct of his expedition. He was the first to introduce fit hill men from outside the area on to an expedition. He was the first to arrange official sponsorship, set up contracts with newspapers and to arrange a contract to write the 'expedition book'. He also introduced crampons into Himalayan climbing thanks to Eckenstein, and a lightweight silk tent weighing only one and a half kilograms, as designed by Mummery and forever thereafter named after him.

Conway lectured about his achievements all around the country, attending dinners and various functions in his honour. Within three years he was given a knighthood, became president of the Alpine Club (1902–1904) and

Fanny Bullock Workman and Dr William Hunter Workman.

in 1905 was awarded the Founder's Medal of the Royal Geographical Society. He lived out his remaining years as a prominent authority on mountaineering and the Karakoram to which he owed so much. We, in turn, owe so much to him.

During the following forty-five years several other explorers and climbers visited the area from time to time including the American couple Fanny Bullock Workman and her husband Dr William Hunter Workman. Mountaineering in the Karakoram had been, by and large, a British preserve and the human landscape was predominatly masculine, until, in 1898, Fanny

Bullock Workman burst upon the scene and continued to do so periodically on seven more occasions until 1912 when Fanny was fifty-four and William sixty-five. By then they had walked more of the Karakoram and climbed more of the mountains than any other visitor to the region. Fanny was a self-assured, rather imperious New Englander. Her father had been governor of Massachusetts and sent Fanny off to finishing schools in New York, Dresden and Paris where she became proficient in German and French. She returned home to marry William, a Yale and Harvard educated surgeon who first introduced Fanny to climbing. Within two years of marriage both their fathers had died, passing on to their children an enormous inheritance giving them total freedom to travel without any financial constraint.

There is no doubt they were a phenomena, going on one cycle tour after another around Europe for five years before spending two years cycling around India. It was towards the end of that period in 1898 that they visited Srinagar, developed a passion for the Karakoram, and made plans to launch a full-scale expedition the year after and, as a result, became completely hooked on exploring the peaks, passes and glaciers of the region. They recorded all that they saw and surveyed in well-illustrated volumes.

They did, in later years, visit the Siachen Glacier region with experienced surveyors whose results were far more accurate than in the region of the Biafo and Hispar glaciers. In all the regions they visited in the Karakoram their illustrations proved generally very useful, even if subsequently their measurements in the Biafo and Hispar region proved to be incorrect. They managed to keep everyone guessing for quite a few years over their specula-tion that Conway's Snow Lake, at the head of the Hispar and Biafo glaciers, was something similar to a polar ice cap, 300 square miles in area, and that their 'cornice glacier' had no outlet.

The Workmans climbed several peaks during their two visits to the moun-tains surrounding the Hispar and Biafo glaciers. One they named during their 1899 expedition after themselves and another after their deceased child Siegfried. They also climbed a peak to the north of the Hispar Pass which they called Biafo Hispar Watershed Peak and calculated its height as being 6,508 metres or 21,350 feet. Most of the heights they made were overestimated and on the 1939 Shipton map Watershed Peak has been down-sized 2,000 feet to 19,310 feet (5,885 metres). However, Watershed Peak was a fine vantage point from where Fanny confirmed her suspicions, deduced during their 1903 visit, that the 'cornice glacier' was without an outlet and if so was a unique feature in the mountain world, however, this was shown not to be so by Bill Tilman in 1937. She also caught sight of 'the Peak B15 23,914 feet which ten years ago on our ascent of Biafo we named Kailasa'. This is the peak that Conway first identified from the Hispar Pass and named the Ogre and now, for no reason known, Fanny arbitrarily renamed it thereby adding to the general confusion.

One regrettable result of their journeys was their harsh and demanding attitude towards the local hill men. Together with their Kashmiri helpers and other lowland servants their behaviour to the Balti villagers was often arrogant and sometimes threatening. According to Kenneth Mason in *Abode of Snow*, 'some of the trouble experienced by later travellers can be traced to this unsympathetic attitude of the Workmans'. Mason quotes Bruce who made a poignant observation on foreigners' expectations: 'what would have happened 100 years ago in Switzerland, if a whole village had been ordered to send every available man with some unknown Englishman and to stay with him for a fortnight above the snowline?' This, of course, is what we, to this day, demand of the Balti villagers who, if treated reasonably and above all with respect, will prove to be just as loyal and reliable in a crisis as the Sherpa of Nepal.

There is a good account of Fanny in *Game Faces* (2012) by Thomas H. Pauly in which he recognises the Workmans and their forthright condescension towards 'inferior cultures' but he also makes the valid point that Fanny's attitude to the porters had much to do with her exasperation at their low regard for women. Fanny was motivated, in part at least, to prove to the world that women were equally capable even when it came to climbing high peaks in the Karakoram. Actually, she also seems to have been very competitive towards any other women who threatened to outpace her. Nevertheless, she can hold her head up high since now she is regarded by most in the mould of her contemporary Gertrude Bell, and later Freya Stark.

John Auden, after a brief visit in 1933 to the Biafo Glacier in an attempt to unravel the confusion of nomenclature of the Ogre, wrote an article for the *Himalayan Journal* in 1934. He inserted a footnote with interesting information he had acquired from the Survey of India regarding the measurement of peak 23,900 (the Ogre) and adjoining peak 23,440 (Latok I): 'The positions of peaks 23,900 and 23,440 were fixed by observations from the following trigonometrical stations: Marshakala (eight miles north of Skardu), Thurigo (seven miles east-south-east of Skardu), and Kastor (twenty miles south-east of Skardu). We are indebted to Lieut. Sams, R.E., of the Survey of India, for this information.' Unfortunately no date is given for when these measurements were made but it is most likely they were taken by Godwin-Austen who climbed several peaks in the Skardu area with his surveying equipment, including Marshakala, Thurigo and Kastor.

Right: Eric Shipton and Bill Tilman. Reproduced by kind permission of the Alpine Club Photo Library, London.

Following the explorations of the Workmans, there were several high-powered expeditions, both scientific and mountaineering, to the Karakoram centring mainly on K2. In 1909 the Duke of the Abruzzi led the first of many great Italian expeditions into the Karakoram. Unfortunately the Duke was dogged by incredibly bad weather but was able to thoroughly reconnoitre K2 and reach a height of 24,600 feet (7,500 metres) on Chogolisa. Negrotto greatly improved upon the maps of the area and Vittorio Sella returned with a set of timeless black and white photographs of all the peaks in the vicinity that have inspired mountaineers ever since. In 1913 the final link was made between the British and Russian triangulation of their respective spheres of influence and cartography. Kenneth Mason played a key role in completing this task, details of which can be found in the *Records of the Survey of India*, Vol. VI., 1914, 'Completion of the link connecting the triangulation of India and Russia 1913'.

In the same year, Arthur Neve, Tom Longstaff and Maurice Slingsby explored the east Karakoram and in particular the Siachen Glacier. In 1913, just before the outbreak of World War One, the Italian Filippo de Filippi, who had been with the Duke of Abruzzi, achieved some very important survey work with a highly scientific expedition covering the fields of geophysics, geology and meteorology. After World War One another husband and wife team arrived and again spent several seasons in the Karakoram. They were the Dutch couple Dr Philips Visser and his wife Jenny Visser-Hooft, who made the first of four expeditions in 1922, exploring mostly in the east Karakoram. In 1929 the Duke of Spoleto led another scientific expedition to the Baltoro and Panmah glaciers as well as to the Shaksgam. In 1930 Professor Giotto Dainelli visited the Karakoram. He had been geographer and geologist on Filippo de Filippi's Italian expedition of 1913–1914 and conducted a thorough geological survey of the Siachen Glacier from source to snout on skis.

In 1937 Eric Shipton and Bill Tilman were in the Karakoram exploring and mapping with the surveyor Michael Spender and the scientist John Auden, who was making his second visit. Curiously, both Spender and Auden were the brothers of famous poets. They were in the area for four months, self-sufficient, surveying vast tracts of the Karakoram mountains and glaciers. During this period, Tilman and two Sherpas headed off to the Snow Lake, now known as Lukpe Lawo, to solve the mystery as to whether or not it was an ice cap. Tilman was able to show that it was but a normal glacier if somewhat wider than most but of only thirty square miles, one tenth of the estimate made by Conway and the American duo, Fanny and William Workman. He then marched on down the Biafo Glacier until he turned west to cross the Sokha La to descend the Sokha Glacier to Dabadas and so to Arandu. As a result of this journey Tilman was able to solve another riddle dreamt up by the Workmans who had thought the Sokha Glacier, which they had originally named the 'cornice glacier', had no outlet. Tilman revealed it was just a regular glacier with a river running out of its snout.

Eric Shipton in his book *That Untravelled World* wrote about this event. The Workmans' categorical statement that this glacier had no outlet caused quite a rumpus at the RGS as sides were taken, with some contentiously thinking it was an unique geographical phenomenon. Shipton wrote of his notoriously misogynistic friend:

> Bill, though unlikely, perhaps, to be actuated by motives of chivalry, always delighted in a chance to confound the scientific sceptics, and had been very anxious to confirm the Workmans' unique discovery. He was disappointed, therefore, to find that the topography of their glacier conformed to the normal pattern. Some years later I found in the archives of the Survey of India the sketch map that he had made on his remarkable journey: the areas representing the 'Snow Lake' and the 'Cornice Glacier' were titled respectively 'Martin's Moonshine' and 'Fanny's Fantasy'.

Two years later Shipton returned to the Karakoram with Peter Mott, Dr Scott Russell, Campbell Secord, Eadric Fountaine, Inayat Khan and Fazal Ellahi. The surveyor general of the Survey of India had strongly recommended Shipton include two Indian surveyors in the party, especially Fazal Ellahi. It was fortunate that he did so for this brilliant surveyor helped produce a very accurate and detailed map of the Biafo and all the tributary valleys and glaciers including the Uzun Brakk Glacier. Peter Mott wrote an interesting and very detailed paper for the September 1950 *Geographical Journal* of this 1939 Karakoram survey that was brought to an untimely end by the war. In his article he refers to the Ogre having been originally designated '18/43m' by the Indian survey of 1855–1860.

PART 2

8 **The Climbers**

The 1939 Shipton map, published by the Royal Geographical Society in 1950, has proved so useful to all expeditions visiting this area, particularly those intending to climb the Ogre. The first expedition was a team from Sheffield, led by Don Morrison, who had broken the logjam after a decade-long ban on climbing in the area. Morrison (1929–1977) was a successful builder, a part-time mountain guide in Canada and ran a climbing school in Zermatt. He was well known in the Peak District for sponsoring the Edale Fell Race, known locally as the Don Morrison Memorial Edale Skyline Race.

The Yorkshire Karakoram expedition of 1971, including also Trevor Wright, Gordon Hibberd, John Gregory and Clive Rowland, marched up the Biafo Glacier around to Snow Lake to check out the north side of the Ogre. They were discouraged after days of wading, sometimes chest deep, in melting snow. They returned down the Biafo to explore the south side of the Ogre where the majority of the team were not optimistic about their chances. Clive Rowland however identified what he thought might be a likely route up a 4,000-foot spur, in appearance rather like the old Brenva route up Mont Blanc. Clive thought it would be a reasonable means of gaining the West Col, a wide plateau of snow, at approximately 21,000 feet (6,400 metres). From the plateau it appeared to him there were several alternative ways to the summit. Unfortunately, his enthusiasm 'to have a look' was not shared by other team members so they marched out and home.

The Japanese, as elsewhere in the Himalaya, came to this area in force, though their first visit was a three-man photographic reconnaissance from Rikkyo University in 1971. They investigated and photographed the south and the north sides of the Latok mountains and the Ogre. This was the precursor to two Japanese expeditions that attempted the Latok mountains in June 1975 but without success.

Don Morrison made a return visit to the area also in June, determined, once again, to climb the Ogre. His team consisted of Pat Fearnehough, Dr John Minors, Alan Burke, Peter Jennings and Ted Howard. The 1975

The 1971 Yorkshire Karakoram expedition. L–R: Don Morrison, John Gregory, Trevor Wright, Dr Hidyar Ullah and Dave Marshall. *Photo:* Clive Rowland.

Yorkshire Karakoram expedition, had to give up, still four days from their intended Base Camp, on the Uzun Brakk Glacier because of appalling labour relations. The three-day walk from Dusso, in good weather, had been trouble free up to Askole where they paid off the Dusso men and took on local porters. After another three days' march they arrived at the camping ground of Ho Bluk where the porters would go no further unless their pay was doubled and they were given more expedition clothing.

Being unable to meet their demands the porters were paid off and the team attempted to relay the loads to the Ogre Base Camp themselves. They soon realised they would not have time to do this and climb the mountain. They returned to Ho Bluk where they split into three pairs to climb three peaks between 18,000 and 21,000 feet (5,500–6,400 metres) in alpine style. The underlying problem that Morrison and others identified was that the Pakistan authorities were simply not prepared for the sudden influx of expeditions into Baltistan. It might have been different if the Karakoram Highway, then under construction, had been completed. Instead, there were delays of up to three weeks flying into Gilgit and Skardu where most expeditions were further frustrated by finding some, if not all, of their baggage missing, for which many

British regimental insignia on the cliff face in the Khyber Pass.

more days were wasted waiting.

The onward jeep or tractor and trailer transport to the roadhead at Dusso was also in short supply as were the number of porters available. That situation was, at least, manageable, but the problems expeditions experienced at the last village of Askole were horrendous. It was all a question of supply and demand, and the demand for porters was, at the time, huge. Apart from the Japanese on the Latoks there was also an American blockbuster expedition to K2 that had commandeered 650 porters. They were reputed to have paid double wages and yet the leader, Jim Whittaker, in total frustration at demands for even higher wages, started to burn rupee notes in front of the striking porters.

Unable to bear the waste of money the porters continued their march to K2. There were also fifteen French climbers on Gasherbrum II, twenty Poles on Gasherbrum III and a small British team on Trango Tower. There was also a small American team on Lopsang Peak. Dennis Hennek, the leader of this expedition, succeeded in climbing the peak in alpine style despite the fact that 'the sudden opening of the region brought a flood of expeditions that were taxing the limited facilities. The porters took full advantage of

The Ogre (right) and Ogre II from Choktoi Glacier.

the seller's market. We therefore had trouble with the government, the local Balti people, our liaison officer and poor weather.' There is no doubt the Balti, rooted in the land, living in isolated mountain settlements and ground down in rural poverty, were not slow to take advantage of the situation – and who could blame them?

I took a first tentative step towards the Ogre in the spring of 1968. I felt the need to go off climbing on the really big mountains of the world following on from my experiences in the Hindu Kush with friends from the Nottingham Climbers' Club in 1967. I started to hatch plans to go overland to Pakistan with Dave Nichol and also Ian Clough. Ian suggested I invite Don Whillans to come along as leader. I wrote off to the Pakistani authorities exploring the possibilities of climbing on Gasherbrum III, Kunyang Chhish and the Ogre. The Ogre was top of the list as I'd just read an article in *Mountain Craft* by Dennis Gray who had marked it up as a better proposition than Trango Tower. Unfortunately permission was not forthcoming but I remained interested.

In February 1969 I wrote to Jimmy Roberts at Mountain Travel in Kathmandu, enquiring if he thought there was a chance of not only climbing in Nepal but also Pakistan. Jimmy had recently been there trying to gain permission for the Ogre. He decided against it on account of the turbulent political situation for this was the time when the young politician Zulfikar Ali Bhutto was gaining strength and support to oust Pakistan's second president and first military dictator, General Ayub Khan.

The Pakistani authorities would only issue permits a couple of months before a team was due to arrive, which was perhaps a major factor in deterring Jimmy from pursuing his climbing ambitions in Pakistan. He therefore recommended I concentrated on climbing a peak in Nepal, where the government had just recently brought their seven-year ban on mountaineering expeditions to an end, and politely suggested this should be after I had done my own research. Really I was grasping at straws as my domestic circumstances, at the time, were unfortunately in a state of turmoil and precluded any long two to three month expeditions. After the Hindu Kush expedition in 1967 it would be five years before I was in a position to go 'off with the boys' again on long trips.

In July 1975, Clive Rowland, Rob Wood, Tony Watts, Bob Wilson, Ronnie Richards and I travelled out to Pakistan to climb Sosbun Brakk, a shapely peak near the head of the Biafo Glacier. We came out on a shoestring budget and with limited time enforced upon us by commitments to jobs back home, and in the case of Ronnie and I, to get back in time to join the South-West Face of Everest expedition (see the account of this trip to the Karakoram in my book *Up and About*, pages 358–360).

We flew out on Afghan Air to Kabul. At £180 return it was by far and away

The Ogre from Ho Bluk on the opposite (south side) of the Biafo Glacier. The ridge on the left skyline is the West Ridge above the West Col.

the cheapest air fare we could find. We then took buses from Kabul, through Jalalabad and the Khyber Pass to Rawalpindi. There we stayed with Buster Goodwin, once Colonel Eric Goodwin of the Indian Army, who had settled in Rawalpindi after a lifetime of service mainly amongst the Pathans on the North-West Frontier. In fact Buster, within a few minutes of meeting, sold us all a copy of his book *Life Among the Pathans*.

Numerous climbers have stayed in Buster's bungalow, looked after by his adopted family. His carers were a rather indifferent couple and the house had seen better days. Buster, too, was past his best at eighty-four and would drift off into soliloquies about his mother. When he came to, he was quite lucid, taking quite a liking to Rob Wood, telling him he was just the sort of chap he would have welcomed into his regiment. Apart from his mother the one thing that Buster seemed to be missing of the old country was cheese. Our supply reduced during the night; at first we thought it was being taken by rodents, but it turned out to be our host. We gave Buster a whole round of Stilton cheese with our thanks and left this charming relic of the British empire for the hills with high ambition.

We were, as can be imagined when considering our time and financial

The south side of the Ogre and Ogre II.

constraints, doomed to disappointment, especially as there was an added factor ensuring our demise – the weather. That year there had been considerable dumps of spring snow on the Biafo Glacier and we simply could not reach our objective. After three days of wading through thigh-deep snow, sometimes up to our chests, we gave up on our peak and turned the trip into a recce of the Ogre. We had already seen the upper part during our journey up the Biafo and now, with Clive's local knowledge, we went back down the Biafo and turned left up the Baintha Lukpar Glacier on to the Uzun Brakk Glacier. We climbed some way up the peaks to the west of the Uzun Brakk from where we had excellent views of the south side of the Ogre.

There was far too much snow, and the team, already depleted with the departure of Bob and Tony for work commitments, and without time to fully acclimatise, were not able to reach any of the attractive peaks hereabouts. The visit had not been a waste of time as far as Clive and I were concerned. Clive was able to reaffirm his commitment to climb up on to and along the West Ridge of the mountain and I became hooked on attempting the magnificent South Pillar of the Ogre – a prow of granite, 3,000 feet high, above which mixed rock and ice climbing led up to a final 800-foot tower.

The Ogre: summit detail.

I had for the last few years, and especially after climbing Asgard right on the Arctic Circle of Baffin Island, thought about climbing big rock walls at altitude. Without any obvious plan in it I had taken to climbing big rock faces, first in the Alps and Dolomites during the 1960s, then in the 1970s in Norway including the Troll Wall, and in Yosemite Valley on El Capitan. These climbs had involved ever-more technical difficulty, and on the big walls on Baffin Island there was the added challenge of subzero temperatures. The next logical step could be right here on the Ogre.

I was now familiar with the effect of climbing in the rarefied atmosphere up to 27,000 feet (8,230 metres) on Everest but, that had been on relatively easy, non-technical snow slopes. Even so, I knew enough to appreciate that to survive at that level it was essential that everything that had to be done was second nature. It would be an interesting exercise, to say the least, to see if I could put the two together successfully: climbing steep rock high in the thin cold air at 23,000 feet. If that worked out I might just have time, before old age and decrepitude, to attempt the mighty West Face of Makalu up to 27,000 feet, and even the highest rock face of them all, the West Face of K2.

My only regret was that I had not started my high-altitude apprenticeship earlier. There is a relatively narrow window of opportunity to climb technical routes at altitude. It can only realistically happen after a climber has accumulated big-wall climbing experience and also climbed at extreme altitude but early enough to ensure that he is still fit and strong enough to put it all together to make technical climbs up high.

Clive and I decided to launch an expedition together for the summer of 1977 hoping that the mountain would still be unclimbed. It had already been reported in *Mountain* magazine that an eight-man Japanese expedition had attempted the Ogre in the summer of 1974. The climbers were from the Shizuoka Tohan Club and were led by Reisuke Akiyama. Team members were: Yukio Katsumi, Kimio Itokawa, Masamitsu Urayama, Tetsuji Furuta, Mitsuo Nishikawa, Takeshi Tsushima and Toshio Kasai. They set up base camp on the Uzun Brakk Glacier and attempted the South Face but an avalanche left two members seriously injured and essential items of equipment lost.

In 1976 the Asagiri Alpine Club (Tokyo) expedition of seven climbers led by Tadashi Nishihara, including team members Muneo Ueda, Hideki Yoshida, Hideo Yamaguchi, Masahiro Murashima, Toshikazu Suzuki, Takeshi Ogawa, made a determined attempt also from the Uzun Brakk Glacier. They climbed the South-West Spur reaching the West Col (20,670 feet/ 6,300 metres) on 12 August. Two days later they climbed the West Ridge to a shoulder at 21,851 feet/6,660 metres but gave up in favour of trying the South Face. By 25 August they had traversed the snow band to the point where it connects with the South Face (21,326 feet/6,500 metres). Incredibly, after being so well poised to at least climb the South Face, their application for an extension to their permit was turned down by the Pakistani authorities and so they retreated.

The Team

Clive Rowland (b.1943) was born in Sheffield and after leaving school started work in a Sheffield steel foundry. He had, by then, already started climbing in the Peak District and North Wales, along with Ted Howard, Tanky Stokes, Paul Nunn and other young climbers who all joined the Alpha Club. This was a club without rules or committees being simply a club that anyone could join if everyone already in it approved. If so, the newcomer was invited to pay a one-off subscription.

Clive was only fifteen when he climbed across the *Girdle* of the West Buttress of Cloggy with Ted Howard, and still in his teens when he led *Brant Direct* and *Unicorn* down the Llanberis Pass. He and the Alpha lads went off to the Alps and the Dolomites and, without much of an apprenticeship, were climbing the Bonatti Pillar on the Dru, the Walker Spur and the Andrich

Clive Rowland.

Fae route on the Civetta in the Dolomites. There were, as usual, epics on early climbs as when on the Yellow Edge of the Tre Cime, Clive and his partner Tanky watched in horror as Graham Evans decided to leave the climb by abseil. Abseiling blind over an overhang Graham became stuck on the end of a rope – thirty feet out from the rock. The mountain rescue team arrived, but, by the time they lowered him down to the ground, he was dead from suffocation.

Clive is justly proud of the ascent he made with Bob Toogood up the North-East Pillar of the Scheideggwetterhorn. This turned out to be only the second ascent overall and the first continuous ascent of this 6,500-foot grade-VI route. In 1973 Clive and Martin Boysen went climbing in Norway up near Nordkapp, where they made the first ascent of The Fortress by two routes on perfect gabbro.

A year later Clive was with Paul 'Tut' Braithwaite, Guy Lee and me on the summit of Pik Lenin via a new route up the North-East Ridge. It had been another epic trip with earthquake and avalanche and with two of our original team knocked out with acute mountain sickness on the Krylenko Pass. Clive physically supported Paul Nunn over the pass at 19,000 feet while Tut helped Speedy Smith who had become delirious, frequently wandering off route while Guy Lee and I found a way down newly avalanched slopes to the valley floor and safety.

Mo weighing in the loads with our liaison officer Aleem.

After our expedition to the Ogre, Clive and his business associate John Smith opened an equipment shop in Inverness. He continued climbing well into the 1980s, including the Cassin Ridge on Denali over five days with Joe Brown and Mo Anthoine in 1986. Just before Mo succumbed to his brain tumour, Clive joined his expedition to the North-East Ridge of Everest in 1988. Not many people know of Clive's achievements in the mountains since he is genuinely modest and 'just can't be bothered with all that media crap'. He will always be known as a fine mountaineer who selflessly helped Chris and me down off the Ogre.

Julian Vincent 'Mo' Anthoine (1939–1989) was born in Kidderminster where his father was a carpet designer. Mo was not so tall but he was extremely well built with a barrel chest – he once stood in for Sylvester Stallone on a film shoot in Israel along with Joe Brown. He developed into a powerful rock climber, repeating many of the hardest routes during the 1960s in North Wales and putting up one or two of his own such as *The Groove* on Llech Ddu. He went on a two-year grand tour hitch-hiking down to Thailand and then on down to New Zealand and Australia with a professional boxer from Derbyshire, Ian Cartledge, known as 'Foxy' on account of his red hair.

In Australia, Mo worked in a blue asbestos mine that was, most probably, the cause of his death from a brain tumour twenty-six years later. It is known that asbestosis and related conditions can show up many years after exposure. In those twenty-six years he packed in a lot of climbing, first in the Alps where he survived a horrendous six-day storm on Mont Blanc when six other climbers perished. He went on to make the first British ascent on Fitz Roy in Patagonia, Roraima in Venezuela and Trango Tower in the Karakoram the year before the Ogre.

He always said about climbing, 'Every year you need to flush out your system and do a little suffering'. Paradoxically his trademark was that climbing had to be fun and one had to stay in control. To that end, he was not averse to using fixed ropes on winter climbs in the Alps and in the Greater Ranges.

Mo avoided publicity and largely funded his expeditions from making the Curver ice axe and the Joe Brown safety helmet, both of which became enormously popular. He will be remembered for helping to keep the anarchic element in mountaineering from being swamped by commercial pressures and the showbiz celebrity culture.

Mo was like François Rabelais (1491–1553), always extravagantly humorous, robustly outspoken and often coarsely indecent – Mo could have been a student of his or even vice-versa. He used his talents to attack the new orthodoxy creeping into climbing, being the main iconoclast – a rebel against conformity. As he lay dying in hospital, visitors would arrive in his room to find him lying there in bed, cross-eyed, tongue hanging out and making grunting noises that had his friends thinking he hadn't got long left, until Mo shot up in bed grinning 'Fooled ya'. Such was his sense of fun, repartee and honesty that 500 people turned up at his funeral in Nant Peris in August 1989.

Paul 'Tut' Braithwaite (b.1946) was born in Oldham from where he started rock climbing on Chew Valley gritstone outcrops. He was soon hooked on climbing, moving from UK climbs to the Alps, at each stage pushing himself to the limits. He has made some twenty first ascents in the UK including *The Cumbrian* on Scafell's Esk Buttress and *Scansor* on Stob Coire nan Lochan in Glencoe, plus scores of technical mixed winter routes on the high mountain crags of the British Isles. In the late 1960s and early 1970s Tut and his compan-

Paul 'Tut' Braithwaite.

ion Richard McHardy were two of the leading rock climbers of the time.

Over in the Alps Tut made many first British ascents including the Croz Spur, winter ascent of the Walker Spur and Shroud Direct on the Grandes Jorasses, the Couzy Pillar of the Droites, Grand Pilier d'Angle on Mont Blanc and numerous first solo ascents of major Alpine routes. In 1971 he climbed the north faces of both the Eiger and the Matterhorn, and the Central Pillar of Frêney, Mont Blanc. The following year he climbed the East Pillar of Mount Asgard on Baffin Island and in 1974 made the first ascent of La Punta Innominata in Patagonia. The same year he climbed the North-East Spur of Pik Lenin in the Pamirs.

Tut will forever be remembered along with Nick Estcourt for climbing through the steep rock band on the South-West Face of Everest in 1975; but for the storm which took Mick Burke, the pair of them could so easily have summited the mountain. In 1976 he made an alpine-style ascent of the Cassin Ridge on Denali and later that year the first ascent of the East Face of Mount Kenya and the first winter ascent of the mountain's Diamond Couloir.

Chris jumaring up our climbing rope en route to the final tower.

I was fortunate to climb several of these routes with Tut, who, like Clive Row-land, was always rock steady, happy in his own skin and utterly dependable.

He started his working life by setting up a painting and decorating business before opening up the successful Paul Braithwaite Outdoor Sports. He sold that on to start Vertical Access, a company which he built up that developed rope-access techniques for working on high-rise buildings. Everything he did, he did well, moving out of climbing into the very dangerous sport of eventing where he attained high standards and several trophies before jumping saddle into the extreme sport of downhill mountain bike racing. In 2006 he came second in the World Vets Downhill Championships at Sun Peaks, Canada.

He is a former president of the Alpine Club, and a trustee of the Nick Estcourt Award and Community Action Nepal.

Chris Bonington (b.1934) was born in Hampstead, London, and educated there until leaving for Sandhurst where he was commissioned into the Royal Tank Regiment. He later spent two years instructing at the Army Outward Bound Mountain School (OBMS). In 1960 he made the first ascent of Annapurna II with a joint Anglo-Indian-Nepali expedition.

In 1961 he left the army and in the same year was on Dennis Davis's expedition that made the first ascent of Nuptse. Also in 1961 Chris was on the first ascent of the Frêney Pillar on Mont Blanc and the year after he made the first British ascent of the Eiger North Face. Not only had Chris by his early thirties pushed the limit of climbing in the Himalaya and the Alps, he had also notched up a number of impressive ascents in the UK, for example the Old Man of Hoy in the Orkneys and *Coronation Street* in the Cheddar Gorge. Chris went on to become one of the three most successful expedition leaders of the twentieth century along with John Hunt and Charles Evans.

He led expeditions to Annapurna South Face in 1970, Everest South-West Face in 1972, and again to Everest, this time successfully, in 1975. There is not the space to list all the many climbs and honours Chris has received – so many that in the *Who's Who in British Climbing* the editor devotes five pages to Chris's achievements; he has in any case just written his fourth autobiography, *Ascent*, to bring his life and times up to date. The one characteristic that always stands out for me is his utter enthusiasm for climbing and his understanding and appreciation of all those kindred spirits who push themselves to the limit. Chris apart from many other obligations is a trustee of the Nick Estcourt Award and the patron of Community Action Nepal.

Nick Estcourt (1942–1978) was born on the south coast, educated at Eastbourne College, University of Cambridge, and then took time out volunteering his services for a year in Sierra Leone.

He moved up to Manchester to take a job as a systems analyst and also to be at the centre of British rock climbing. His parents introduced him to hillwalking in the Lake District and later to the Alps where he climbed with guides they hired for him to reach high peaks. By the time he entered Cambridge Nick was already a competent rock climber and was elected president of the Cambridge Mountaineering Club. In the Alps he went on to make fast ascents of the Walker Spur amongst others and made the second ascent of the South Face of the Fou and a first ascent of the North-West Face of the Pic Sans Nom in 1967.

Not only was Nick a very competent mountaineer but he became an essential member of Himalayan climbing expeditions being conscientious and hard-working. His support was essential to Chris Bonington when leading the Annapurna South Face expedition of 1970 and the Everest expeditions to the South-West Face in 1972 and 1975.

I was pleased that Nick was on our Ogre expedition as I had spent a few excellent days with him pushing out the route on the South-West Face in 1972. In 1975 it was Nick and Tut who led the crux pitches of our South-West Face route which paved the way for Dougal and me to establish Camp VI and later reach the summit.

Nick Estcourt.

He lived life to the full – parties, pub, repartee and arguments about every-thing– yet he never lost his basic humanity and remains forever for me the most honest man I ever met.

We were crossing a snow basin together on the West Ridge of K2 in 1978 when windslab snow broke off with us on it; down we went in the avalanche until the rope snapped leaving me on the edge of a 3,000-foot steep wall. Nick plunged on down, lost in thousands of tons of avalanche snow debris.

Originally, on the 1977 Ogre expedition, we were four with Clive asking Mo Anthoine to join him, and me asking Dougal Haston on the way out from our climb on the South Face of Denali. I put it to Clive that we should invite Chris Bonington and also Tut Braithwaite as he was quite keen on climbing the pillar. Clive was all for having Tut join us as he was more comfortable with northern people from a working-class background and more reticent with those from the higher echelons of society. I had my own personal reasons for asking Chris, and to persuade Clive, I pointed out that his presence would make life easier when it came to organising food, equipment, flights and dealing with the embassy and authorities in Pakistan. I invited Chris on this expedition, not only because we had developed a close friendship, but also out of gratitude for the three expeditions he had organised for me and others – to Changabang and twice to Everest. I also thought it would be interesting for Chris to experience the kind of expedition my friends and I were more used to.

On 17 January 1977 Dougal went off late in the afternoon to ski down a couloir on the Riondaz above his home near Leysin. He was found the next morning buried under avalanche debris where he had suffocated to death. This was a massive blow to all of us that knew him well and in particular to Chris and me who had climbed with him most recently and who were so looking forward to climbing with him again on the Ogre – who better to have on the first ascent than Dougal from Scotland? It was, after all, the Scots who had done so much to gain access into the north-west of India, indirectly paving the way for our attempt.

With the death of Dougal, Clive suggested that we invite Martin Boysen to take his place. Since it was most likely that Chris would be climbing with Dougal, Chris had, after Dougal's death, already thought to ask Nick Estcourt along, with whom he had climbed on numerous occasions, and had a very close relationship. Clive, who had already put this invitation to Martin, now had the onerous task of letting him know that a replacement had already been found. Charlie Clarke was invited along as doctor and volunteered to handle all our food procurement and the organisation of it up to Base Camp.

We now had an interesting and experienced team. Mo had recently been on two expeditions along the Baltoro Glacier attempting to climb the Trango Tower which he managed to do in 1976 with Martin Boysen. They reached the summit after a long siege of a highly technical climb in mostly bad weather. Mo arrived on our expedition with filming equipment as his application to compete in the first Mick Burke Award had been accepted.

Nick was also filming but only for Chris. He had signed up to promote Bovril who had asked him if it would be possible to take film of him speaking into camera during the expedition to the Ogre but without mentioning the Ogre specifically.

I had hoped to climb the Ogre with as little fuss and bother as we climb in Europe, North America or the Andes, and definitely without the encumbrance of film gear, fixed ropes, radios and obligations to major sponsors. Now Chris was lined up to appear in television advertisements for Bovril and, if we agreed to have it filmed on our expedition, then they would give the expedition £3,000. I had let it be known to other members of our team that I would rather we were not involved. What Mo actually said about that was not printable, but basically he was saying that I was silly not to take the money and the consensus was to accept the offer – so we did.

Chris knew that this would be quite a different sort of expedition to the last three big expeditions he had previously led. He had written telling me that not only was he looking forward to climbing in alpine style but was also eagerly anticipating going on a trip with far fewer responsibilities. I suggested there would not be a leader and that in general, and as much as possible, we would avoid the 'ordeal by planning' as Tilman once put it. The approach, I implied, would be entirely laissez-faire where, when a job needed doing, we could rely upon the right man to step forward and do it without the bother of rotas.

In actual fact, at different stages of the expedition leaders would emerge naturally to attend briefings with the authorities, hire porters, pay porters, sort out Base Camp and the distribution and preparation of food and equipment. Although it might appear to lack organisation, everyone would be involved at different times, when appropriate, depending on personality and experience. Just because I had gained permission for this expedition to climb the Ogre I was determined not to assume the right to lead it, any more than Clive or anyone else. Clive and I had probably performed the most important function when we had invited the others to join us. It only remained to be seen if our confidence in the team working together, in a spirit of mutual aid, was justified.

9 **March to Base Camp**

On 23 May 1977 we all met up in Rawalpindi. Clive and his friend Jim MacDonald, from the Black Isle, had driven all the food and gear overland in a white Ford van generously loaned to us by David Hooley of the main Ford agent in Nottingham, Hooley's Garage. We went off for the expedition briefing at the Ministry of Tourism as Clive and Jim told us of their epic journey, all of which will appear in Clive's memoirs. Pakistan was, when we arrived, going through another period of political upheaval which was resolved on 5 July during our expedition when General Muhammad Zia-ul-Haq seized power in a bloodless revolution.

One of the many requirements of an expedition at that time was to have a doctor. This was something we now did not have as Charlie Clarke, for personal reasons, had withdrawn. Nick had taken on catering duties but we still lacked a medic. We had thought of elevating Mo to 'doctor status' since he knew a lot about mountain rescue; he said he would put on a white coat and stethoscope for the meeting and we could brief him on technical names for common ailments liable to occur in the mountains. Streptococcal bacteria were mentioned in relation to sore throats: 'No problem,' said Mo. 'I can remember "strapacocktome" and I will ask him how his jugulars are doing as well!'

Mo's ribald sense of humour was never far from the surface. He told us not to worry because if he failed to convince the Ministry of Tourism he would insist that Chris was our doctor as he had received so many honorary doctorates from all over Britain. Mo contributed to the trip at this point not only by dispensing gallows humour at every situation but also in gaining us access to the British Embassy Club with its well-stocked bar and large swimming pool overhung with huge bushes of marijuana.

During the Trango Tower expedition Mo and the other members had been rescued from a fleapit in Rawalpindi and persuaded, without too much trouble, into the British Embassy Club. They stayed with Caroline Weaver and other embassy staff in their spacious air-conditioned apartments.

Polo tournament at Skardu. *Photo:* Nick Estcourt.

Our British Ogre expedition was also made most welcome. For Clive and me it was such a contrast to our previous billet in Rawalpindi at Buster Goodwin's rundown hothouse of mosquitoes and rodents.

Some of the team joined the embassy Hash House Harriers on their weekly evening run over the nearby hills; this was not only a help towards integration with the embassy staff but also good preparation for our walk in to Base Camp. Chris and I managed to fix up an appointment with the British ambassador, John Bushell, to discuss our intentions to climb on K2 the following year. We wanted to enlist the ambassador's support for our campaign to secure permission to pioneer a way up the West Ridge of K2; this was something we had heard that Jim Whittaker's American expedition was also intending to climb. The ambassador said he would support our preferences when next in contact with the Ministry of Tourism and with Mr Awan (Deputy Minister of Tourism) in particular. The briefing at the ministry was, as it happened, uneventful. The tourism department bent over backwards to help our expedition get off to a good start; not having a doctor in our team was brushed aside with a vague suggestion that we could always seek medical help from the Americans on Trango Main Tower who had brought two doctors.

The rest of the journey in to Base Camp was, in comparison to previous years, a breeze. The concerned authorities in Pakistan had really taken to heart much of the criticism that had been levelled at them and had rectified many of the problems. Perhaps the most important of these was to set

Dusso: the start of the trek until a new Jeep road was pushed up the valley to Askole by 1990.

reasonable salary structures when it came to hiring jeeps, tractors and porters; at least now we had a yardstick to compare our costings and to argue our corner if it became necessary. We were certainly helped by having an excellent liaison officer in Captain Aleem who remained with us throughout the expedition as a kind and sympathetic member of the team.

It was such a relief to have to wait only one day this year to fly from Islamabad into Skardu as opposed to the seven days we had waited in 1975. We did however have to hang around another two days for the baggage to arrive and it took eight days from Skardu before we arrived with all our gear in Dusso. To be stuck in Skardu once is not a bad thing as this historic town has several attractions. Excursions can be made up to the fort on the commanding heights above the town or across to the carving of the Buddha on granite boulders at Satpara. We were lucky to be there that year to watch a polo match between Skardu and neighbouring villages. After a very physical tournament, Skardu, the home side, were the winners, with the local sheikh, police and army chief applauding.

Above: Registering porters at Dusso.

Right: A Karakoram oasis – wherever there is flat ground and water there is life, otherwise the Karakoram is all mountain desert.

On 4 June we set off from Dusso with our caravan of porters to arrive three days later in Askole. This part of the journey was down in the Braldu River valley – the river that drains K2 – where periodically we passed through villages set in oases of fields, green with ripening wheat, mulberry trees laden with fruit, stately poplar trees and dog rose in full bloom. In between the settlements of adobe houses it was desperately hot on the open bare hillside. There was some relief, just before Askole, where we were able to soak and refresh ourselves in pools of warm geothermal water, gurgling up from subterranean sources.

After being awoken by the mullah calling the faithful to prayer we purchased *atta* (flour) from the headman, Haji Mehdi, who also helped us take on more porters. Despite the fact that a large Japanese expedition had just passed through on their way to K2 the cost of flour and porters did not seem to be that inflated. For all their remoteness the people of Askole were used to European, American and Japanese mountaineers, mainly bent on climbing K2. Now other mountains were becoming available to climbers. Already the British and French had climbed Mustagh Tower way back in 1956. The Austrians climbed Broad Peak in 1957, the Italians Gasherbrum IV and the Americans Gasherbrum I in 1958, and the Americans again climbed

Top: The porters earn every rupee they are paid for such heavy and dangerous work.

Above: The hot geothermal sulphur springs thirty minutes' walk from Chongo and our last bath for many weeks.

Stately poplars.

Masherbrum in 1960. After that there was very little climbing in Pakistan until the early 1970s.

Surprisingly, the day after arrival we were able to set off up the Braldu as far as Korophon where we turned north-west on to the snout of the Biafo Glacier. It helped that three of us had been to Askole twice before and Mo three times. It was especially important that the liaison officer had been well briefed at the ministry as to the salary structures and also the recommended stages and number of resting days. Our first-aid box was also well used and helped convince the villagers that we were on their side by treating them with the same care as we treated ourselves. We were now, as far as Clive and I were concerned, on familiar ground, camping first at Namla (c.12,000 feet) where we saw bear tracks, then Soblong (c.12,500 feet) where we were joined by a friendly dog, and finally on 9 June, late at night, we arrived at Base Camp (c.15,500 feet) just off the Uzun Brakk Glacier.

One other useful result of our 1975 recce was to discover, right at the end of that trip, an acre of pasture nestling in the triangle between the two coalescing side moraines of the Baintha Lukpar that leads up to Latok II and the Uzun Brakk Glacier coming down from the Ogre. To come across

Haji Mehdi, the headman of Askole, who became over the years a good friend.

this triangle of lush, green grass covered in alpine flowers, buzzing with insect life and with a clear freshwater stream gurgling through it, in the middle of this wilderness of rock and ice where the soils are thin and growing things scanty, was simply wonderful. It was also protected from the mountain winds by the converging moraines on two sides and by the rocks below the Ogre's Thumb on the other. Returning two years later, it seemed the glacier had moved down about 100 metres (unless, of course, our memories had failed). Clive, with help from Chris, went out on to the moraine-covered Uzun Brakk Glacier and recovered the cache of gas, tents, ropes, etc., we had left in 1975.

Already ensconced nearby were members of the 1977 Yorkshire Karakoram expedition led by Don Morrison, on his third visit to the area. There were, by coincidence, now four of the lads into climbing retail, as Don had recently opened equipment shops in Sheffield and Liverpool. He was soon comparing notes with Clive, Tut and Nick who were all into the climbing retail business. The other members were Pat Fearnehough, Pat Green, Tony Riley and Paul Nunn. Paul told me later that Don was deeply disappointed not to have been able to book the Ogre but was pleased to have secured as compensation Latok II (23,320 feet/7,108 metres), a worthy replacement.

Only in the remote areas and in the Hunza valley are women to be seen in this land of Islam.

It was like being back camping on Snell's Field in Chamonix, with everyone knowing each other for many years from climbing in Britain, the Alps and the Pamirs in the case of Paul, Tut, Clive and me. With so many people now at Base Camp, including the two liaison officers and the small band of porters being retained for a few days to move stores up to Advanced Base Camp, there were environmental concerns.

Pat, a college lecturer in food hygiene by profession, came across a porter straddling the stream with his pants half up, too embarrassed to move, as the sahibs remonstrated 'no shitting in stream'. Mo told him, 'Chris Sahib has already told you about that', referring to Chris who, two days previously, had given a directive to the porters in general: 'No one must shit'. When this was translated the porters looked surprised and a little alarmed until Chris relieved the situation, so to speak, by going to the stream demonstrating, 'See absolutely no shitting in stream – shitting okay over moraine.'

All of the Balti we came across were strong characters.

Nick, being ultra-careful and forever fretting that the food would not last the expedition, was fair game for Mo's humorous interventions. In a little hut the porters built, one of their number, Jack, cooked for the two liaison officers and also helped Nick cook for us. Jack now wanted ghee, the local butter. Nick told him in his immaculate public schoolboy English that the porters already had extra ghee and that it really would not last at this rate of consumption. Jack looked confused.

Mo piped up, 'Ghee gone'. 'Okay sahib,' said Jack and walked across to see what the two liaison officers wanted to eat. Nick told everyone that the food could not last if we kept feeding everyone at the current rate. Finally Nick's agony came to an end when he was off up the mountain and free from kitchen duties. The day before his departure, he announced, much to Mo's and everyone's amusement, 'At midnight tonight I am absolved from all further cooking'.

'Hard times ahead,' said Mo.

By 08.20 the sun was up and a caterpillar had crept over the threshold of my tent. A brew came over from Clive's tent accompanied by the strains of Rod Stewart telling us for him it was late September, although actually for us it was a lovely spring day on 13 June and the meadow had just come to life with the last of the winter snow melting away fast – time to go climbing.

Clive and I, after searching our memory banks, had already found a

Above left: There is evidence of inbreeding and also of iodine deficiency resulting in quite large goitres that restrict movement of the head. *Above right:* Life is hard at Askole, 10,000 feet above sea level, where temperatures remain subzero for up to four months of the year; consequently life expectancy is relatively low.

reasonable way through the lateral moraines and séracs to a safe site for Advanced Base Camp. During the next few days we set up and stocked Advanced Base Camp and started to organise for our various routes. Mo, Clive, Chris and Nick prepared to climb up the South-West Spur. The Japanese had sieged it the previous year, up to and a little beyond the West Col.

Tut and I made several carries from Advanced Base Camp, up steepening snow into a loose gully, giving access to a platform at the very foot of the South Pillar where we made our cache of food and equipment. Included in the gear was a special hanging tent, designed by Hamish MacInnes and me, and manufactured by Blacks of Greenock. From the cache the pillar beckoned as it clearly offered superb climbing up granite cracks right on the prow, not unlike sections of the *Nose* on El Capitan. Finally, we were ready to go and left Advanced Base Camp with food for fifteen days, enough to keep us going while continuously climbing up to the summit but with reserves to weather the odd storm. The hanging tent should, just about, take bad weather out of the equation.

I had thought of a design change to accommodate an idea of having the hanging tent permanently erected even as it was hauled up the vertical granite from one belay station to the next. I had talked about this new concept at Base Camp thereby foolishly opening myself up to Mo's ridicule. 'You could leave Tut inside, just pull him up still in bed,' and 'Bring the missus

Top: Leaving the ablation valley to cross the Biafo Glacier.

Above: Porters resting at the entrance to the Baintha Lukpar and Uzun Brakk glaciers and our first close view of the Ogre in 1977 – to the left is the Ogre's Thumb and to the right, in cloud, Ogre II.

The Ogre with the entrance to the Uzun Brakk Glacier.

and kids next time and haul them up.' I had gained the confidence to plan for this two-week alpine-style push from an experience while sitting on the rim of El Cap in 1973. I had met the Canadians, Steve Sutton and Hugh Burton, still with seventy kilograms of food and fuel left over from the eight days they had just taken to climb a new variation finish to *Mescalito*.

On the way back up the steep gully of broken rock I jumared the final section on the climbing ropes we had left hanging from the cache. I managed to dislodge a rock which rattled down the gully below. In horror I watched it ricochet off the gully wall and slam into Tut's thigh. It didn't break his femur but he was in great pain with every step. It took two days to descend to Base Camp, where he was out of action for at least a week as I sat feeling mortified that I was responsible.

After two weeks of waiting for a large bruise and maybe a blood clot to dissipate, Tut was still finding walking painful, never mind rock climbing. It was such a crushing blow literally and emotionally for Tut and yet he remained philosophical, shrugging it off as just one of those things. With a heavy heart, and with some help from Tut, I started to recover the food and equipment from the base of the pillar. So ended a two-year obsession that had caused me to catch my breath a time or two at the thought of just him and me cutting loose and going for it.

Yet again it seemed that another climbing ambition would not be realised. Over the preceding twelve years circumstances had often dictated that it

Above: Base Camp. The triangle of green pasture with a clear freshwater stream running across it made an excellent site for Base Camp, being protected from the valley winds by the two coalescing lateral moraines.

Right: The Ogre south side. Advanced Base Camp was placed on the wide expanse of snow, convenient for the prominent South Pillar and the South-West Spur on the left.

Over page: The Ogre from the air, showing the Uzun Brakk Glacier curling up from the left, around the Ogre's Thumb and up to the South-West Spur leading to the West Col on the left side of the Ogre. The upper half of the South Pillar can be clearly seen in this photograph, as can the final summit tower. *Photo:* Galen Rowell.

seemed the climb would not be made and the summit would remain out of reach. The usual reasons were the physical and bureaucratic problems of travelling to the mountain, or it would be inclement weather. It might also be disharmony or illness in the team, or lack of experience or, as now, an accident. There were occasions however, when, against all the odds and after letting go of all ambition, the situation changed in favour of achieving the objective after all.

In 1965 in the middle of the Sahara, en route to climb in the Tibesti Mountains, the vehicles broke down in the Murzuq sand sea in a country where the highest ever temperatures had been recorded. All ambition to climb the unclimbed Tarso Tieroko evaporated in the searing heat and drifting sand of that Libyan desert. However, the mechanics worked throughout the night and fixed the lorry, and lowered the pressure in the tyres enabling the expedition to proceed to the mountain and eventually for us to climb Tieroko in good order and by three different routes.

Making plans at Base Camp. L–R: Tut and I intend to climb the South Pillar; Nick with Chris, and Clive with Mo, are planning to climb up to the West Col together.

Similarly, and more recently, I had in the autumn of 1975 decided to return home at the very beginning of the South-West Face of Everest expedition after the death of Mingma, a young mute Sherpa lad who I had befriended. I was accused of being responsible for his death on top of being distressed at his loss and it was all so upsetting that I decided to depart for home. The situation changed as other members of the team helped me rationalise Mingma's death. Also apologies were made and the atmosphere became more conducive for climbing; subsequently, against all the odds, I reached the summit with Dougal Haston.

Only the year after, again with Dougal, this time on the South Face of Denali, the stormy weather was so violent and protracted that I let go of all ambition that year thinking I might try again another day. The weather improved and we cautiously continued, finding a way up steep gullies of ice and across avalanche-prone snow slopes to complete the route which, as always, having not thought it possible, then comes as a gift.

By 15 June Advanced Base Camp was already well stocked with a month's supply of food and fuel thanks to the carries made by six Balti porters and all six team members. On the same day Chris and Nick were the first to occupy Advanced Base Camp and the following day to start climbing up the South-West Spur leading to the West Col snow plateau. After fixing the first two

Top: Advanced Base Camp. From here the expedition divided; Tut and I headed to the rock pillar.

Above: The team at Advanced Base Camp. L–R: Clive Rowland, Chris Bonington, Nick Estcourt, Doug Scott, Tut Braithwaite and Mo Anthoine.

Left: The 3,000-foot South Pillar of the Ogre.

Top: Climbing the loose gully to the start of the pillar. Further up I dislodged a rock that smashed into Tut Braithwaite's thigh, very sadly putting him out of action for the rest of the trip. *Photo:* Tut Braithwaite.

Above: Tut Braithwaite struggling back to Advanced Base Camp after the accident.

Steph Rowland (left) and Jackie Anthoine – the two wives arrived at Base Camp ten days after their husbands, Clive and Mo, and the rest of the team. For a few days they humped loads up to Advanced Base Camp before leaving as their permits were not in order.

pitches the morning became oppressively hot and so they descended to Advanced Base Camp to link up with Clive and Mo. But where were they? Chris wondered, 'Could they still be lolling about at Base Camp waiting for their wives?'

Steph Rowland and Jackie Anthoine had arrived at Base Camp pursued by a posse of armed police. The wives had assumed, wrongly, they were on the expedition permit and so not having a permit they had to use all their powers of persuasion talking their way through one police check point after another, but now, the police on reflection had decided to escort them back down to Skardu. With the support of the two liaison officers the police allowed the wives to remain at Base Camp for the foreseeable future while they sought further clarification from their superiors. It was a situation for which Mo, Clive and I all felt some responsibility. It had not been easy for the girls, especially Steph who was suffering from the sun, and both, being young and attractive, in a very male-dominated society, had found the whole thing most unpleasant. Ultimately, I blame myself as organiser for not thinking to raise the matter at the expedition briefing in Islamabad. So, having met their wives, Clive and Mo left them to recover from the exertions and frustrations of their trek, and that same day went back up to Advanced Base Camp.

10 Climbing the Ogre

On 17 June with Chris down with a cold, Nick and Mo went up the route to push out the ropes towards the site of the first Japanese camp. On the following day Clive and Chris, who was now recovered, climbed over 600 feet right past the Japanese camp while Mo and Nick spent the day taking a rest and filming. On 19 June Nick and Chris left Advanced Base Camp at 2.45 a.m. carrying heavy loads of food and fuel reaching the Japanese camp now known as Camp I in three and a half hours. They descended as Clive and Mo continued above Camp I fixing rope until late afternoon before sliding back down the ropes from 19,500 feet. On 20 June Chris and Nick went up to occupy Camp I from where, during the next two days, they extended the fixed rope to 20,200 feet.

By working a shift system for a week, in various combinations, the four had fixed the way to just below the West Col by 23 June. On that day, Mo and Clive, after ten hours of climbing, returned to Chris and Nick at Camp I with the good news that the climb could now enter a new phase. The first 4,000 feet of the mountain had been climbed and fixed with rope to just below the West Col at 20,630 feet. The climbing had been up classic alpine mixed terrain of steep ribs of snow and ice, interspersed with steps and slabs of granite.

On their return to Camp I, Chris announced that he and Nick had decided that once the route had been made to the West Col they would set off for the summit. Clive recalls Chris's reaction on hearing that they had reached the col as being 'Jolly good! That means that Nick and I can go for the summit tomorrow', about which Nick 'looked surprised and sheepish'.

There had been a breakdown in communications. Chris later revealed his thoughts that, although good progress was being made, 'some rifts in our team were beginning to show. Mo and Clive were altogether more relaxed in their approach and did not have the same sense of urgency that Nick and I shared. We believed that we should grab the good weather and make as much progress as possible, get ourselves established on the col, and then go alpine style for the summit. Mo and Clive, on the other hand, seemed to favour a more

deliberate approach and preferred the idea of going for the West Ridge of the mountain'. (*The Everest Years*, 1986).

This is at odds with Clive's recollections of events at this time. He and Mo had always thought the crest of the West Ridge, from the West Col, would be the most interesting route but during the climbing to the West Col, according to Clive, there had been a change of plan, 'which had been discussed by the four of us, to climb the snowy south face up to the summit block together'.

Clive was put out, saying, 'I thought we were meant to be climbing as a team'. Mo pleaded for a rest day, 'And we can all go up together the day after.' Clive recalled Chris being 'unmoved by our protestations' and was adamant that he and Nick would be heading off for the summit the next day.

Very early in the morning of 24 June, Chris and Nick set off up the ropes for the West Col carrying heavy packs containing food and fuel for a week. Mo and Clive awoke to find they were alone and decided to descend to Base Camp for further acclimatisation, 'disgruntled and sulky' as Mo wrote in the *Alpine Journal*.

Meanwhile down at Base Camp, Jackie, who had done a considerable amount of alpine climbing, readily took up my suggestion that we went and climbed a small rock spire that Clive, Ronnie Richards, Rob Wood and I had attempted two years previously. This was something both Jackie and Steph had always had in mind. In fact, Jackie was hoping to carry out a reconnaissance of a suitable peak to climb in 1978. Steph unfortunately was suffering from the altitude and maybe heat exhaustion. Jackie and I didn't make it due to huge balconies of unstable snow which came crashing down in the afternoon heat, taking my rucksack with them. On our return to camp we came to know that earlier that morning Don Morrison, leader of the Yorkshire Karakoram expedition, had died. Don and Tony Riley were walking along the Baintha Lukpar Glacier following, by then, a well-used track in the snow, when suddenly Don fell through the snow down into a deep crevasse – so deep that Tony could not reach him or hear him above the noise of the subglacial stream.

The first we knew of the 'separatists' up on the South-West Spur was when Mo and Clive arrived in camp that evening. Clive had a set look on his hairy countenance that had us wondering 'what next?' It wasn't so bad, just that they felt 'disillusioned' that Chris and Nick had taken off without a full and frank discussion. It seemed to Mo and Clive that all four of them needed more time to acclimatise, and go down for more supplies especially gas cylinders and more rope. Mo recalled I was 'a bit disgusted' at this turn of events, as related by Mo and Clive on their arrival at Base Camp.

Left: Memorial cairn to Don Morrison. Don fell to his death down a crevasse on the Baintha Lukpar Glacier during the Yorkshire Expedition's attempt to climb Latok II.

Above: Granite slabs at the start of the South-West Spur. Conway's Ogre is on the left.

Right: Looking down the South-West Spur.

I did wonder if this situation had come about due to the fact that Chris and Nick had far more high-altitude experience than Clive and Mo. Mo had never been much above 20,000 feet previously, whereas the two thrusters had been above that height on numerous occasions and up to 27,000 feet on Everest's South-West Face. Clive had been up to 23,000 feet on Pik Lenin so had a better idea than Mo, but still would lack the confidence of Nick and Chris who were totally mentally prepared for the debilitating effects on the body and the altered state of thinking processes that the lack of oxygen brings about. For Clive and Mo, climbing in those realms was still some-thing of a mystery and so naturally they preferred to more cautiously feel their way forward.

There was a further reason for being in Base Camp and that was to check not only their wives but also what Tut and I were planning to do. They deduced from watching our movements that all was not well. Mo succinctly summed up the situation as 'Mountain 1 – Climbers 0' and later proceeded to suggest ways we might even up the score.

During the next few days the card school resumed and the Latok expedi-tion gave up on their mountain and erected a cairn to the memory of Don before leaving. I suppose there is always an element of *Schadenfreude* when these traumatic events happen – to the extent that everyone not directly

West Summit

Main Summit 23,900 feet

Red Pillar

West Col

South Pillar →

← South-West Spur

← Advanced Base Camp

The Ogre: the South-West Spur can be seen on the left leading up to the West Col. Halfway up is Camp I. From the West Col Chris and Nick traversed the cummerbund of snow to the right-hand end from where they gained access to the South Face snowfields. *Photo:* Ronnie Richards.

involved is relieved it wasn't them. In actual fact it could so easily have been any one of us that had previously walked unroped along snowed-up glaciers. Our relief, no doubt, had the positive effect of making us more determined to survive by being more cautious in future. It seemed to me to be a particular waste of a good life; I had known him since I was a teenager working as a temporary instructor alongside the more experienced Don at the White Hall outdoor education centre in Derbyshire. He was a good man, with three children, and who, with his wife Pam, was intending to purchase and run a farmhouse in France. Over the years there had been several such accidents, so devastating for family and friends left to pick up the pieces. I knew that for Pam and her children, life would never be the same again.

On a couple of occasions Tut thought his leg had improved enough for him to have a go at the South Pillar but, after only a few hours walking out of Base Camp, it became obvious to him that his leg was not up to severe rock climbing. The idea of climbing the pillar was now abandoned in favour of accepting Mo and Clive's invitation to join them on their rocky West Ridge route. This would at least give Tut and me some technical climbing. 'Good to have you with us, Crip,' said Mo to Tut.

On 26 June we all went up to ABC accompanied by Jackie and Steph. They too were carrying loads up and they also brought superfluous gear back down to help with the eventual evacuation of ABC. We would not see them again until back in Islamabad.

We had hoped to go from ABC direct to the West Col Camp II but it was obvious that Tut needed to carefully nurse his leg if he was to go all the way to the summit. We all enjoyed the slower pace and the view from Camp I, not to mention the craic. Mo was also able to get more film in the can during this period of exceptionally good weather.

By 29 June, after ferrying gear up fixed ropes, we were well ensconced on the West Col astride the West Ridge. Despite the fact that Nick and Chris were not flavour of the week, we all hoped they were safe and well and, in fact, began to worry as to how they were doing. Chris had left a note for Clive and Mo saying they had fortunately found more Japanese rope for fixing and that they hoped to be on the summit by 28 June. During the next few days we climbed up towards the Red Pillar on the West Ridge. It was so good to be up there where we were now able to see across Snow Lake and the Hispar Pass to all the peaks stretching out to the far horizon including Kanjut Sar, Distaghil Sar and distant Nanga Parbat way round to the south-west.

On 2 July we began to make preparations, at Clive's suggestion, to go out on the route taken by Nick and Chris to see what had become of them since they were now two or three days late. During the night, while sharing a tent with Tut, I distinctly heard Nick shouting 'Tut'. I awoke with a start and could not get back to sleep worrying and thinking of their wives, Caroline and Wendy. I put a brew on wondering if perhaps our concern for them over the last few days was fully justified and they had come to grief. Suddenly there were actual voices; thank God it was Nick and Chris arriving back at 05.30 in the morning.

Nick was absolutely wasted, his nose peeling from the sun and eyes wrinkled beyond belief like Hermann Buhl after soloing Nanga Parbat. Chris was hoarse, and Nick could not speak at all, so I spoke first and told them that Don Morrison was dead. There was some discussion of how easily this could happen to any of us and only then did I ask Chris, 'Have you done it?' 'No,' said Chris. 'Good' said Clive with a twinkle in his eye. Mo laughed de-lightedly! Over brews of tea we came to understand that Chris and Nick had returned from a magnificent, two-man alpine-style, but unsuccessful, push for the summit.

It was only when they were standing in the snow below the final tower that they realised they didn't have the strength, or the food, fuel and equipment, to climb it. As compensation they settled on climbing the steep snow to reach the West Summit of the Ogre. They were now absolutely shattered from their week of hard and difficult-to-protect climbing across rock slabs and slabs covered with just two or three inches of snow, for pitch after pitch – all day until forced by dark to bivouac in snow caves or out in the open.

They had obviously both set off not fully acclimatised, particularly Nick, who had kept going on a cocktail of brews, codeine and Mogadon tablets and was now desperate to reach Base Camp and return home. He did man-age to croak that he was prepared to wait for the rest of us before doing so. Chris, on the other hand, was still full of ambition for the summit, and man-aged to talk us into going back down for more food and fuel having pointed out how technical, and therefore time-consuming, it would be to climb the final tower. Mo was the only one to object, being persuaded 'much against my will' as he thought it was 'a bit bloody stupid as the weather was fine and we had all the gear we needed'. The six of us descended back to Base Camp to pick up more supplies and to give Chris time to recover from his ordeal. Chris later wrote in *The Everest Years* that on meeting up 'I felt uncomfort-able, disappointed at not having reached the main summit and, at the same time, guilty now that we had attempted it and allowed ourselves to be drawn into unspoken competition with the others.'

Looking back to that early morning catch-up at Camp II it seems a matter for regret that we could not all celebrate the success of two of the expedition reaching the West Summit of the Ogre in such fine style. We should also have been giving thanks that there had now been a thorough reconnaissance of the way to the Main Summit.

West Summit
23,700 feet

Main Summit
23,900 feet

Biv V

Biv IV

Camp III

The route taken by Chris and Nick for the Main Summit and West Summit.

It was to the credit of Mo and Clive that after being ditched by Nick and Chris they could so easily forgive the past and accept Chris on to our team. That is not to say that Mo and Clive were not pleased to be descending for further acclimatisation, to see their wives as well as to collect more food, fuel and a bit more gear.

It was decided since time was running out and in order to give Chris, Nick and Tut more time to rest and recover, that Mo, Clive and I would go back up the ropes, first to the West Col snow plateau and then establish a camp at the base of the 1,000-foot Red Pillar. Over the next two days we jumared up the ropes and climbed the steep snow ribs up to the West Col at 20,670 feet (6,300 metres). From there, in baking sun, we plodded up a relatively easy south-facing slope of now thigh-deep snow to the foot of the Red Pillar. We found a reasonable, if exposed, balcony that would accommodate two tents.

Top: Chris leaving the snowfield cutting across the South Face. *Photo:* Nick Estcourt.

Above: Nick climbing up granite slabs covered in ice and thin layers of snow. *Photo:* Chris Bonington.

Right: View of the summit tower from the West Summit. *Photo:* Chris Bonington.

Left: Camp I – Mo, Clive and Tut having a brew at this exposed campsite but safe from rockfall.

Top: Nick melting snow for a brew just below the West Summit. *Photo:* Chris Bonington.

Above: Kanjut Sar (25,460 feet/7,760 metres) from the West Col snow plateau.

Left: Starting to climb the Red Pillar.

Above: Camp III – Conway's Ogre (21,070 feet/6,422 metres) is seen on the near right. Sosbun Brakk, (21,040 feet/6,413 metres) is on the far right. The two rounded summits left of centre are Ganchen and Hikmul.

So far I had done nothing much but hold on to jumars clamped to fixed ropes that I had not fixed, that only required a dull plodding routine to make upward progress. Snow flurries and cold did nothing to stimulate my interest in the climb. In fact, as we put up the tents I would have given anything to be at home with my family – Jan, Mike and Martha. Then only half an hour later inside my tent supping hot tea, I looked out of the entrance as the sun set and decided that there was nowhere else I would rather be than up there at 22,000 feet watching the sun dipping down, silver lining strands of cloud strung out over Snow Lake and the Hispar Glacier beyond. Range after range of bristling mountain peaks stood out silhouetted against one other, the nearer ranges sharply and darkly defined while those in the distance faded into the sun's defused haze of yellow light. Above them all some 100 miles away, Nanga Parbat caught the last of the sun, while everywhere else was plunged into gloom. We zipped up the tent against a strong wind and snuggled content into our sleeping bags.

Left: Camp III with Snow Lake and the Hispar Pass in the distance.

Above: 'Man of the Mountains' Clive Rowland at the top of the Red Pillar.

Above: On the Red Pillar of the West Ridge with the Sim Gang Glacier, Snow Lake and the Hispar Pass in the middle distance.

Right: The West Ridge beyond the Red Pillar. To the right is a 5,000-foot sheer drop to the Sim Gang Glacier.

Mo had unearthed another coil of Japanese static rope which he was keen to fix along with our two climbing ropes. From our Camp III on 8 July, resting up from having left about 450 feet of rope fixed to the pillar, we spotted a lone figure climbing towards us. It turned out to be Chris, who, as he wrote later was, 'worried about my reception'. There had been tension but it was now beginning to evaporate and, in fact, Chris wrote that he 'almost immediately felt part of the team' on arrival. Chris came into camp and we accepted him readily, earning our respect for having gone all the way up to the West Summit of the Ogre, all the way back down to Base Camp, and then, after only a couple of days' rest, was back up at 22,000 feet. He had enormous drive, matched with the constitution of an ox. He is like our Border terrier which, once it has the scent of a rabbit, there is no stopping it; so it is with Chris when the summit is in sight.

Chris had brought up a sack full of much-needed food and the bad news that Tut and Nick had decided to stay down and wait for our return. Tut felt his injury would hold us up and Nick could hardly speak, so bad was his throat, and so emaciated his body. Mo, Clive and I had worked well together, really enjoying the climbing from Camp III up the West Ridge Red Pillar.

Above: West Ridge bivouac. This was the penultimate bivouac before the summit, where we were full of optimism and enjoyed a fine evening supping tea while watching the sun go down.

Right: Clive and Mo leading the way across steep snow towards the West Summit.

In the Alps such a route would be graded très difficile (TD). Here in the Karakoram we were climbing at considerably higher altitudes where time was required between each series of moves just to allow enough oxygen back into our muscles. Chris and I went back down to Camp II for more food while Clive and Mo led up steep gullies above our previous high point to reach an easier-angled snow ridge. Chris found the return trip to Camp III very heavy going, putting in doubt his chances of reaching the summit. We decided to take a day off to give Chris time to gain strength knowing that to make the summit before consuming all the food we would now have to move really fast.

The next day, with the help of the Japanese ropes fixed to half the pillar, the four of us made good time climbing it to reach a snow ridge upon which we could bivouac. Clive and I dug out a platform in the snow for the bivouac tent while Chris and Mo dug out a snow cave. Mo ran out two climbing ropes and fixed them to the crispy snow to ensure a good start on the morrow. We sat resting from our labours supping mugs of tea, watching the sun set, without a breath of wind. We turned in, all of us quite optimistic of reaching the summit in the next day or so.

Left: Mo and Clive enjoying a well-earned brew stop.

Above: Checking out the Main Summit from the West Summit. *Photo:* Chris Bonington.

The following morning we set off across a thin layer of snow hiding hard ice underneath it, over which Clive and Mo led the way before reaching a rocky rib where we had lunch. I then led on, up to the West Summit, where we all sat, having made the second ascent, taking advantage of our bird's-eye view of the final 800-foot tower. It was immediately obvious that Chris's insistence that we should descend to bring up more gas, food and climbing equipment was not just out of self-interest. Had he been less than emphatic we might well have been up there quite 'naked before the mountain' (the title of Pierre Mazeaud's book) – lamentably short of food and fuel to sustain our climb, which was already taking much longer than expected.

By late afternoon we had climbed down 400 feet of soft snow to reach the place where Nick and Chris had made their top bivouac, not so much a cave as a hollow in the snow. We had plenty of time to dig out quite a commodious cave, something which Mo and Clive especially were pleased about since they were concerned that the whole slope might avalanche. So we burrowed deep into this icy part of the mountain, inserting ice screws at the back of the cave from which we tied off.

Chris had been climbing very slowly in fits and starts, and not with his usual rhythm. He had, uncharacteristically, slipped, banging his elbow, while

Top: Chris stirring the porridge in our highest snow cave. Mo and Clive are tucked away in the back.

Above: The final tower of the Ogre.

Right: Chris heading toward the final tower.

West Summit
23,700 feet

Main Summit
23,900 feet

Biv IV

Biv V

Red Pillar

Camp III

The route from Camp III to the summit.

traversing a stretch of the rock pillar. As we were pottering about, in and out of the cave, I put it to Clive we might stand a better chance of climbing the final tower if he and I were again to rope up together as we had been on the 1,000-foot pillar. He agreed with me that Chris was slow and suffering from all his exertions over the past two weeks.

At this point I felt more comfortable climbing with Clive whom I had gotten to know over the last few years while climbing with him in Scotland, the Pamirs, and out here making a reconnaissance of the Ogre two years previously. As a climber he may not have been as driven as Chris, Nick and me, but he was an excellent rock climber given to making sound judgements and basically someone I had always felt confident to be with in the mountains. He let me know he was sorely tempted but replied, 'Nah, I'm sorry youth but I've promised I'll help Mo with his filming', and, as an afterthought, 'We'll be right behind you.'

That evening Mo and Clive occupied the back of the cave while Chris melted snow and I rehydrated four freeze-dried meals of beef stroganoff followed by rehydrated apple flakes and numerous cups of tea. I snuggled into the down of my sleeping bag, well fed and content with the day's climbing. There was time to register, in those moments of calm, after so much effort and frustration, excitement at being in this position, so well placed to be setting off up that final tower for the summit of the Ogre. I felt no anxiety, as I often did while packing my sack the night before a serious climb in the Alps; now there was only curiosity to see how it was up there and how I would manage.

Racking gear for the crux pitches of the climb. *Photo:* Chris Bonington.

Negotiating a hairline crack on the steep headwall, with the aid of pegs. *Photo:* Chris Bonington.

Despite being up at 23,000 feet we all seemed to sleep well. In fact, I hadn't even heard Chris's notorious snoring or him pottering about preparing the porridge until he woke me. Mo and Clive lay in their sleeping bags intending to film from the cave and then catch us up later. Chris set off and I followed in his steps across deep, soft snow. He asked me to lead the steep, mixed ground to the left of the tower. For two rope lengths I found the climbing quite difficult (Scottish IV/V) and it only eased off as I approached the top of a minor pinnacle. We then roped down and across to the main rock tower now only 400 feet below the summit.

To me it was obvious that Chris had not fully recovered his strength from his previous attempt on the Ogre and this was completely understandable –

The wall relented and the cracks were wide enough for free climbing. *Photo:* Chris Bonington.

in fact it was remarkable he was up there at all. I could not bring myself to tell Chris that if he did not hurry up we would never make it. I simply said I ought to lead the next pitch. There was only one day's food left in the cave to see us all the way down to Advanced Base Camp. I knew we could survive several days without food on the descent but we were unlikely to have the willpower, or energy, to have another go at climbing up without food. Chris did not

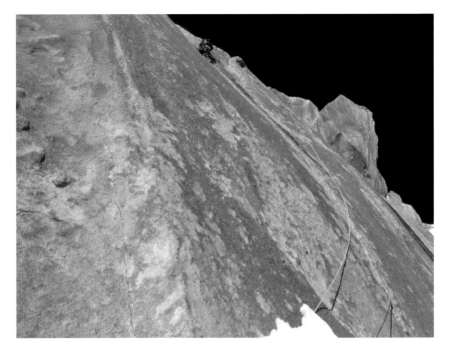

At 100 feet the crack ended in blank rock. I fixed a wire chock and asked Chris to lower me down fifty feet so that I could make a pendulum swing to reach a crack system on the right. On the fifth attempt I managed to enter a crack and climb it to a belay. *Photo:* Chris Bonington.

object. Later, I was surprised to read of his resentment of my 'grabbing the lead', although, at the time, there was no argument and he seemed to reluctantly accept it was for the best. As it was, the ropes got into a tangle and became jammed in a crack which took up another hour of our day.

We climbed a corner of wonderful rough, warm granite for 150 feet, protected from the wind, with a midday sun beaming down – it was a very enjoyable pitch at about VS/5.7 which normally Chris would have romped up in the lead. I traversed across to belay beneath the final blank wall. Chris proffered me the lead with no objection at all. I was now festooned with a whole rack of big wall climbing gear, a range of pegs, wires, hexes and a couple of tube chocks. I followed a crack climbing both free and on aid, mainly from wire chocks. Eventually the crack I was following petered out into a blank wall. I put in a wire as high as possible and asked Chris to lower me down so that I could start a pendulum, swinging from one side to the other, in the hope of reaching another crack system over on the right.

With all the rope out he managed to give me fifty feet, enough to enable me to gallop backwards and forwards until the arc of my swing was sufficient to gain access to the crack. As I was trying to arrange protection I slipped out and went clattering back across the granite. I pulled myself together and, after a rest, repeated the process several times without success. I put in one last

Chris taking out the equipment on the crux pitch of the climb. The weather was calm and sunny and the rock dry, rough granite – the best of conditions for such a pitch. Below is the basin up which Nick and Chris had climbed to make the first ascent of the West Summit.

determined effort, knowing my strength was fading fast and managed to get my hands well jammed in and climb up the crack to where I could place a peg. This crack I got into was less steep but now flared rather like those on the headwall on the *Salathé* on El Capitan. It would still take wire chocks and finger jams and the toes of my Makalu double boots.

I climbed it at grade VI, mainly free with some direct aid that eventually enabled me to reach the top of the wall and a belay on a snow ledge. Chris came up raving about the quality of the climb and the exposure.

It was certainly the hardest climbing I had ever done at that altitude. It had taken place on superb, brown, weathered granite without a breath of wind and with the sun beating down. I found it possible to climb the whole pitch without the encumbrance of gloves. I am sure, had it been otherwise, I would never have made it, not up there at nearly 24,000 feet. There was a final snow gully leading to the summit but to get to it meant negotiating an overhang. Chris made an attempt but couldn't make it.

I had a go, stepping on his back since I was still without crampons. I managed with an almighty effort to reach over the little roof and wedge my shoulder into a recess, and find a finger crack to enable me to enter fully into the gully to kick steps in the snow to the summit. Just as I arrived on the summit, the sun disappeared below the horizon.

On the summit of the Ogre at 7 p.m. anxious to descend to our sleeping bags at the cave bivouac. *Photo:* Chris Bonington.

During the time Chris was coming up to join me, I had time to enjoy being up there in the middle of the Karakoram. In those precious moments alone I had never felt more 'in the mountains' for that was all there was to see – mountains and glaciers – in every direction.

Now, for the first time, the land to the north revealed its secrets – that is, to me, for it was down below that Eric Shipton, Eadric Fountaine and Sherpas from Nepal had spent three weeks during 1939 mapping the glaciers I was now looking down upon – the Sim Gang, Nobande Sobande and the Chok-toi. Between the glaciers were shapely spires, some of them quite sharp, and in the distance fewer than fifty miles away was the magnificent pyramid of K2. A bit closer and just to the right of it, seemingly just as big and impressive, was Mustagh Tower.

Clive and Mo, who had been filming us from a snow pinnacle, had given up on climbing the Ogre for the day having realised how technical it was and that they were now too late to avoid being benighted if they continued. They returned to the cave to try for the summit on the morrow. In two abseils they made it down from the pinnacle back on to the track across the snow.

Chris on the summit of the Ogre.

They left their two climbing ropes fixed to the slope to help me and Chris back to the cave in the dark. Chris was soon up to join me on the summit to enjoy the same panorama of peaks now fading into the evening gloom. It was now seven o'clock on 13 July and we were both conscious of the beckoning darkness and that our sleeping bags and head torches were in the cave.

11 **The Epic Descent**

A miserable cold wind blew in as I left the summit shuffling down an arête of granular snow to fix a sling around a block of rock for the first abseil. Hurrying, with darkness imminent, I forced my cold and aching body down the frozen double ropes in a series of jerks and hops, all the time moving left towards the crack I had climbed some three hours before. The rope just reached the crack where I tried to clip a couple of pegs left in situ – they were just out of reach so I stepped my feet up to hold myself in better balance. Without looking I stepped on to a veneer of water ice that had formed from melting snow in the evening cold. In that careless moment I lost control.

My feet slid across the ice, off into the air and away I went, galloping across the rocks, striding faster and faster, trying to regain control, to arrest the swing but then spinning, rolling wildly round and round and away into the void, clutching the ends of the rope for all I was worth. I twisted and turned in an effort to face squarely, great cracked walls of rock streaked with snow looming up fast – on and on, zooming in, with my boots in front of me like a pair of buffers – no stopping it now.

Splat went my legs, arms and body against the rock with the clatter of gear. Down went my specs and ice axe. I came to a stop, bouncing on the end of the rope, every bone shaken. The surge of blood pumping around my head slowed to a trickle and all was quiet after what seemed like a lifetime of total involvement – time had been in suspension as it does when it is all happening. Luckily I was still conscious for there was no knot on the end of the double ropes. I had come to a halt, hanging free, so I stretched out a toe to push against the rock and swing myself on to a ledge; there was something badly wrong with my left leg as pain shot up it into the groin. I then pushed with my right leg – there was definitely something seriously wrong there as it crackled and gave a sickly sensation of grating bone and unnatural movement.

With the left foot and reaching over with my hands, I eventually manoeuvred myself on to a ledge, hammered in a peg, slotted in two wire chocks and tied myself off. Now the weight was off the ropes I yelled up to Chris to

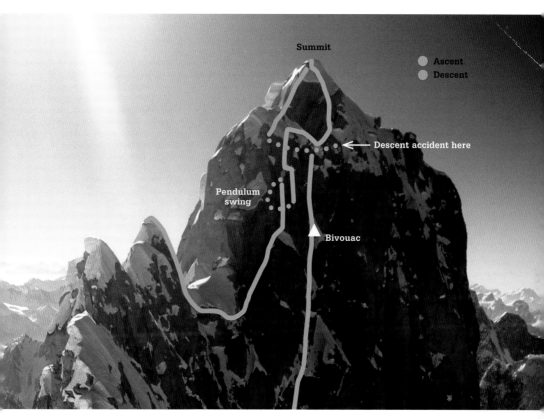

Summit

Ascent
Descent

← Descent accident here

Pendulum swing

▲ Bivouac

Diagram showing our route up the summit tower and the scene of the accident.

come on down. My initial reaction had been fairly rational as there was much to do and occupy my mind, but now, in waiting for Chris, I realised I had messed up and that we were unlikely to reach the snow cave, sleeping bags and a brew that night. Clive later wrote that down at the cave:

> At 8 p.m. I was lying in my sleeping bag and it was almost dark.
>
> 'I'll just go out for a final look to see how they are doing, before I tuck in,' Mo announced.
>
> He was standing in the cave entrance, when 'Oh God! No! He's gone!' he screamed.
>
> 'What? Who's gone?' I yelled. I didn't want to know, fearing the worst.
>
> Joining Mo at the entrance, we could just pick out two figures in the gloom, about 140 feet apart.
>
> 'It's Doug,' Mo replied.
>
> 'What's he doing down there?' I asked Mo.
>
> Mo said, 'He was just reaching the west end of the terrace to

Looking across to the West Summit: Mo and Clive are on the West Ridge, from where they retreated intending to make their ascent to the summit the following day. The line of tracks in the snow lead to the snow cave. *Photo:* Chris Bonington.

where he would abseil from, when I don't know what or why it happened, but he just sort of fell off. I can't understand it, that was just a walk.'

Mo later said: 'He suddenly shot off into space and I remember my knees buckled, Clive sank down saying "Oh God, no" and then there was silence. Then I heard a few moans and groans and confused shouting from Chris, then the very clear voice saying "I think I have broken my legs". I tried shouting up but got no reply … they were too engrossed … so back into the snow cave … no climbing gear … a bit bloody helpless … a bloody awful night … thought of broken femurs … staring at the roof of the cave, cursing inwardly.'

Chris abseiled down and, as he appeared above my head, I told him I thought I had broken both my legs; he told me not to panic, that I wasn't going to die! 'We'll get you down somehow – whatever happens.' I thanked him for his encouragement and told him that I certainly had no intention of dying. He pulled the ropes down, fixed the next abseil and disappeared into the gloom below. As I watched Chris disappear, down the double ropes now pencil thin with his weight, I had more time to take stock of the situation and knew there would be new rules for winning.

I never doubted I would get off this mountain, not with people like Chris, Mo and Clive to help, but exactly how it would work out I had no idea. I knew I was now in a very difficult position so it may seem a bit odd that I experienced feelings of exhilaration at all the uncertainty I had created. I was impatient to get moving, not only because I was beginning to freeze but also to get to grips with this new situation and try to solve it. The ropes came slack and I slid down them with my back against the rock to join Chris on a snow patch in the middle of the tower. It was a relief to know that at least I could abseil.

Chris had hacked out most of a long ledge in the snow down to the ice. I made the mistake of stepping on to it only to collapse in agony. I then went down on to my knees and helped Chris enlarge the ledge with both of us chipping away with our ice picks. We spent a very cold night having left the cave wearing only jumpers and windproof suits – plus underpants and socks of course! After my night out with Dougal below the summit of Everest this was the coldest bivouac I had ever experienced, as it was for Chris. We sat opposite each other throughout the night – occasionally rubbing each other's toes to keep the frostbite at bay. We had neither food nor drink, only snow to suck on. It did occur to me that if I was going to do something as stupid as this I could not have been with a better person than Chris to help sort it out and I told him so.

When you are exhausted, benighted up at 23,000 feet, on a vertical rock tower and having to get your partner on to a ledge, with his two broken legs, that task can only be achieved if everything that has to be done can be done as second nature. Chris had that experience and so, despite our very exposed position, Chris's handling of the ropes was such that I never felt in danger of toppling off the ledge. Unbelievably, he lived up to his reputation of being able to sleep most of the night anywhere and did so, snoring away at times in between waking up to gently rub life back into my freezing feet and for me to reciprocate.

It was a long night waiting for the first light of dawn which was ages coming. There was no wind, no sound at all, just a penetrating cold kept at bay by involuntary shivering and creating friction heat by rubbing arms and legs. Finally, after nine long hours there was the realisation that the sky had become a shade lighter. One benefit of such a totally unplanned bivouac was that at first light we simply got up and left – without the annoying job of stuffing sleeping bags into sacks that never seem big enough.

After several more abseils down the frozen ropes, we reached the snow and Chris traversed over to meet Mo and Clive, who were approaching digging out large bucket steps as they came. Chris continued across to the cave while Mo and Clive got the stove going to produce a very welcome brew.

Left: Chris digging out the entrance to the snow cave which had become blocked in the storm.

Above: Clive and Mo took charge of getting me up to the West Summit and down via the rocky West Ridge, to the West Col and 4,000 feet down the South-West Spur.

It was 6 a.m., as I crabbed across towards the cave, with my knees stuck into the line of steps, now practically a continuous snow ledge. Mo and Clive patiently kept me on a tight rope for the next two hours. Knowing I would be resting up all day in the cave, and feeling guilty that they had not managed to reach the summit, I did suggest they went for it now, to which Mo said 'You must be joking' – or words to that effect!

By eight o'clock we were all ensconced in the cave eating up the last of the freeze-dried meals and catching up on lost sleep. So far so good I thought – at least I can abseil down steep rock and crawl over soft snow. We were looking forward to moving out the next morning, now without the weight of food and the gear that remained on the summit tower.

Up to then the Karakoram had enjoyed very favourable summer weather, but, on the morning of 15 July, Mo awoke at the back of the cave suffocating as the entrance was now blocked with fresh snow. We broke out of our insulated shelter to a maelstrom of swirling snow that went on and on at the same furious rate throughout the day. Clive went out into the storm trying to find a way up to the West Summit 400 feet above us with Chris belaying from the cave entrance. They soon returned with their clothing plastered in snow and Clive's beard encrusted in ice. The snow was thigh deep, angled at fifty-five degrees, and so it was a case of one step up and two back to the cave to see what the morrow would bring. Clive had only managed to gain a height of eighty feet. We had discussed descending down the route Chris and Nick had taken the week before, but when all the pros and cons had been aired we decided to retreat by the way we had just climbed. Now, with all the fresh snow lying and maybe avalanche-prone on the rocks and icefields below, descending the West Ridge was confirmed as the only option.

During the night the storm increased in violence, blocking the snow cave entrance again. With Mo muttering something about 'Karakoram storms don't last long' he went outside to find the same howling blizzard still raging. This was becoming a real problem – apart from not having any food, if we stayed up here at 23,000 feet we would only deteriorate physically. Clive set off to try again for the West Summit with Mo belaying him from the cave entrance. Clive pulled out all the stops and, after three hours or so, succeeded in reaching the summit. It had been a brilliant effort and dangerous too as the powder snow was very prone to avalanche down 10,000 feet to 'death alley' between Ogre I and Ogre II. Mo followed, tying loops in the rope so I could haul myself up with Chris pushing me from behind. Nearing the top I ran out of steam and so Clive and Mo yanked me bodily up the final seventy or so feet.

It was there, on the West Summit, we caught the full blast of the wind viciously blowing spindrift into our faces. By the time I arrived Mo and Clive had disappeared. I had a mild panic thinking Chris and I were now on our own, and me without a sleeping bag and mat, which Clive was carrying. Suddenly there was a very welcome shout from below announcing they had fixed the first of many abseils that would take us continuously off the mountain. Oh me of little faith! Mo went down, fixing abseils one after another, which in those conditions took all day and into the night.

With at times nil visibility, Mo had demonstrated what a fine mountaineer he was and a natural when it came to route finding. He fixed three abseils, ending up in the middle of the steep ice slope he had led on the way up. Mo then stood waiting for me for three hours on the tiny ledge he had chopped out of the ice, supported by Clive and Chris, all the time wondering if his numb toes were now frostbitten. He located the traverse that led to the snow cave that he and Chris had dug five days previously. Again I had coped with the abseiling but it was on the traverse that I slowed everyone down, despite the handrail that Mo had fixed, as I could only crawl dragging my broken legs. Feeling guilty about this I dived into the cave to help dig out the drifting snow. Before it was properly finished it was pitch black outside and temperatures had plummeted so that everyone piled in to a space tight for two men. It was the worst night of all; no food, wet, still above 23,000 feet and me, painfully slow and slowing them down with the Red Pillar to come.

Right: Crawling down from the West Summit towards the top of the Red Pillar. Clive can be seen in the picture, Mo had gone ahead fixing abseils. Chris kept me on a tight rope while taking this photograph. *Photo:* Chris Bonington.

Very soon the storm intensified, making the descent more difficult. *Photo:* Chris Bonington.

Next morning, Mo emerged from his soaking-wet sleeping bag to check conditions and announced, in his deadpan Birmingham accent, 'If anything the storm is worse'. Mo had slept in the entrance along with Chris. Chris had been given a sleeping bag cover of a new fabric to test. It was Gore-Tex and it worked – his bag was dry and Mo's sopping wet. Clive followed Mo, I followed Clive and Chris brought up the rear – all of us bent on reaching the tents at Camp III. Not to make the shelter of the tents was unthinkable as we would have a desperate night sitting in slings clinging to the rocks of the Red Pillar as there was no place to bivouac.

I avoided becoming discouraged and overwhelmed by not thinking of the problem as a whole, or wallowing in comforting thoughts of Base Camp or, for that matter, Camp III. To solve a big problem I found it best to nibble away at it, one feature at a time, not one day at a time – such as that knob of rock looming out of the snow and mist, or crossing the next snow basin to the ridge of snow on the far side. Achieving these limited goals, one after the other, seemed to keep my spirits up. Adopting this 'one feature at a time' approach helped me stay focused on making certain I didn't damage my legs, especially the right one, any further.

The one worry I did have was that I might be inflicting permanent damage that would curtail my climbing and rugby, perhaps bringing my playing days

Starting to descend the Red Pillar. *Photo:* Chris Bonington.

to a premature end. That thought, too, had to be managed. If I became too paranoid about that possibility, I would completely immobilise myself and, after all, the main thing was to keep moving down – the ultimate aim to be back home. There were times when I was resting, my hands and knees pressed into the snow, when I would have comforting thoughts of home with Jan and the children. I even planned a kitchen extension! There were other times when I would shut my eyes and see caricature images of people I knew, my father for instance, in lederhosen shorts held up by lilac-coloured braces with his short back and sides haircut, smartly parted, pushing a pram telling me not to worry. Mo was always on hand with his black humour to help prevent any 'poor me' thoughts developing into continuous self-pity.

The area of the descent that was most painful was, surprisingly, crawling across fairly level ground where I was liable to catch my boots on protruding rocks. It was only on steep, completely snowed-up rock faces that I felt comfortable, for then Mo would have fixed up the abseil ropes and I could slide down with my body making contact with the mountainside while my feet stuck out into space – away from obstacles.

In this fashion I started to descend the Red Pillar with the help of Clive and with the rope arranged by Mo. It was at the start of our descent at the top of this very exposed pillar, with the snowstorm as turbulent as ever, that both

On the Red Pillar, where Chris later smashed his ribs. *Photo:* Chris Bonington.

Chris and I nearly reached the foot of the mountain involuntarily in just a few seconds. Mo was doing his best to link up with the ropes fixed to the bottom half of the pillar. To reach them he had set up ropes for abseiling. There had been a lot of shouting which I hadn't understood as I abseiled down the double ropes. In the storm, I hadn't noticed one end of the double rope was shorter than the other, so, as I came off two ropes on to one, I shot off down, out of control. I instinctively threw an arm over a short length of rope that Mo had providentially fixed horizontally across the pillar and stopped.

I was badly shaken but my legs were no more painful than before. Despite my earlier misgivings, the fact Mo had put in that length of rope saved my life. Clive shouted up to Chris, the last man down, that the ropes were uneven and, as a precaution, Clive tied off the end of the long rope to a spike. Chris also failed to hear the warning, or notice the disparity of rope length, and shot off the end of the shorter one falling twenty feet before hitting a rock against his chest and stopping. Had Clive not thought to tie off the end of the rope Chris could well have plunged to his death. Cold and getting colder there was no alternative but to carry on with the descent. Fortunately Chris was relatively pain free immediately after the accident. It was only later, down at Camp III, that the severity of Chris's injury to his ribs became

Looking down the Red Pillar towards Camp III barely visible on the snow.

apparent, and that he had probably also broken a bone in his wrist.

Mo had arrived at Camp III first to dig the tents out from under three feet of snow; he had to completely re-erect them as they had been flattened by the storm. Chris and I, with Clive safeguarding us down the final part of the pillar, arrived into camp after dark. What a relief it was to crawl straight into the tents, out of the tearing wind, and into our sleeping bags. For me it was a long painful process to remove frozen canvas gaiters, boots, inner boots and socks so that I could bring my frozen toes back to life. At the time I was more concerned with my frozen finger ends which were definitely frostnipped from crawling around all day in wet gloves.

Mo did a fantastic job in finding a way down in the white-out conditions, never having to back track. He had to be inventive with the abseil anchors as most of the pegs and slings had been either left or lost at the scene of my accident. Mo chopped short lengths of rope off the main climbing rope, made slings out of them and draped loops around flakes of rock or around chockstones wedged in cracks.

The storm was more violent than ever during the first night back at Camp III. Huge dumps of snow pressed the tent down on to the occupants. The two fittest, Clive and Mo, had to go out into the storm to shovel snow

Above left: Clive in the tent suffering from frostbitten fingers and toes. *Above right:* Playing cards with Mo while listening to Dr Hook on the tape deck. *Photo:* Clive Rowland.

off the tent and, in the process, their fingers became frostbitten. We could only imagine what state all of us would have been in had we been forced to bivouac in the open on the Red Pillar.

Mo came into the tent Clive and I were sharing to warm up as his sleeping bag was now reduced to a useless clump of wet soggy feathers. Both Clive and Mo were quite worried about the condition of their digits, especially their toes, which were definitely frostnipped. We played cards and Dr Hook on the tape recorder. We had eaten no food for three days but we did have a tape recorder that Mo had brought up for his film. The only problem was we only had one tape – I shall never forget 'Sylvia's Mother' and the 'Queen of the Silver Dollar'.

Chris was now in a bad way – coughing, his throat hoarse, his voice down to a whisper – and every cough increasing the pain under his ribs. He burst into our tent the next morning announcing that he really must go down as he thought he had pulmonary oedema. The rest of us were keen to see the storm out in the comfort of the tent, particularly Mo who quizzed Chris about his condition. There did not seem to be any gurgling noises from his chest that are said to afflict those suffering oedema and, as Mo pointed out, Chris had been high so often and had never suffered much in the way of acute mountain sickness previously.

Mo's conclusion, put in his inimitable way, was 'Don't worry, Chris, it's probably only pneumonia!', and added that it wouldn't be helpful to spend any more time out in the swirling spindrift. Despite the fact that Mo had just announced he had not felt his toes for nearly a week, and that all of

Clive's digits were also numb, and despite it being our fourth day without food, we decided to give it one more day. We had found a box of sugar cubes and a pile of used teabags in the snow with plenty of life left in them, so we were assured of a dozen more brews.

We also found a scattering of Oxo cubes lying in a corner of the tent that Clive and I were sharing. Mo came over to our tent for music, cards and to let us know that, in his opinion, Chris also had plenty of life left in him yet. 'He just woke up, turned over in his sleeping bag and told me, "we are going to make a fortune out of this". I asked him how and in a fit of coughing he said "The Book! – The Book!". Clive and Mo were incredulous. I have to say that at the time I was not so keen on this book idea, being embarrassed to have made such a mess of things!

It was still blowing hard the next morning as we descended to the West Col snow plateau. It was there in crossing the snow I found that being on my hands and knees was actually an advantage in the deep snow and I was able to do a bit of trail breaking. At our former Camp II site on the plateau, two feet down in the snow, we dug out a plastic bag which had been used for waste; from the bottom Mo and I scooped out and ate the frozen boiled rice from a previous meal which was now mixed with cigarette ash.

Mo rummaged around and found an ounce of milk powder and in another bag three packets of fruit sweets and two packets of cough sweets. We shared them out when Clive and Chris arrived. I crawled off carrying Clive's pack as he had to go and recover a tent that had fallen off it higher up. There was now about half a mile to go across the snow but, at last, the clouds were rolling back to reveal the mountains all around sparkling with fresh snow right down to the glaciers. As I crawled past Mo, sat in the snow, he reached out with a smirk on his face and clipped bunches of climbing gear on to Clive's pack thinking I would not notice him adding insult to injury. However, Clive was catching us up and caught this callous act on his camera.

All that day we descended the fixed ropes down to the glacier where we were finally safe – comparatively safe that is – for it was here that Clive sent me ahead to check for crevasses! I protested. Clive said that I was expendable being so damaged and Mo said I wasn't worth saving anyway! It was this black humour that had done more than anything to lighten the situation in which Chris and I had found ourselves. Chris was now in a very bad way, coughing up orange-coloured phlegm and clearly in far more pain than I was, made worse by not knowing exactly what was wrong. It was clear that he had not only broken a number of ribs but there were also complications which were hard for us to diagnose. Having broken ribs playing rugby, and again after being thrown off a horse, I knew how painful it can be not knowing where to put yourself, sitting on the edge of the bed all night unable to find

Down on the West Col snow plateau, with me carrying a sack for the first time, crawling past Mo who adds climbing gear to my load *Photo:* Clive Rowland.

a comfortable position, and for Chris to have to down-climb and abseil must have been so painful – yet he never complained.

It slowly dawned upon us that Advanced Base Camp was no more: no tent, not even a box of food or equipment – nothing there but bare ice. No one seemed that bothered, possibly because Advanced Base Camp had become a rather grim place after all the snow had melted. It was simply one more thing to take on board, although it did register as being a bit strange.

I found it most difficult when having to traverse across steep rock. *Photo:* Clive Rowland.

Chris jettisoned his gear as he walked down the glacier towards the moraine, including a camera which Mo salvaged and a fleece jacket which I gathered up and tied around my waist. The two of them forged ahead with Clive keeping me company on to the bare ice and moraine which we reached by late afternoon – now with only three miles to go. The others had given me their overtrousers which helped cushion me from constant wear and tear on my knees from the boulders and gravel of the moraine. It was now the eighth day since breaking my legs; eight days of trying not to damage them further with the help of the others.

Now only Clive was with me, sauntering patiently along behind, as I worked steadily, down on my hands and knees, crawling around boulders trying to reach Base Camp that night. Clive decided to go ahead but I pleaded with him to stay for I could not face making that last couple of miles on my own – the strain was beginning to tell. I had brought such an iron will to bear on managing my predicament and I now seemed to be faltering with Base Camp just around the corner. Clive pointed out that it would soon be dark and it would be quicker if he went ahead to get a head torch and food.

After eight fraught days on the Ogre, now safe crawling down the upper Uzun Brakk Glacier towards Base Camp. *Photo:* Clive Rowland.

So I crawled along slowly, on my own, into the night, able to pick my way as it was a clear starry sky.

After an hour or two Clive came back with food and said, 'You are never going to believe this. Tut and Nick thought we had all died so they've buggered off'. We scoffed down muesli bars and cubes of sugar as I crawled on to Base Camp in the dark with Clive guiding the way. Chris was in his sleeping bag on the moraine with a burning gas stove – the only light available. At half past three in the morning Clive spotted the light, and, so it was, nine days after the accident my companions had got me safely into Base Camp.

When I arrived I had worn right through four pairs of overtrousers to my bare knees which were bloody and swollen like melons. Chris was there telling me in a hoarse whisper that only I could have found the strength to have made it. It was kind of him to say so but I knew in reality any one of us would have done the same. To be up there in the first place you have to be fit and strong and since we all wanted to get home again all of us would have used our strength and willpower to have done so.

Back at Base Camp: Clive is trying to ease the pain that Chris is suffering from badly smashed ribs.

We were surprised to find Chris on his own. He explained that Mo had shot off down the valley in hot pursuit of Nick who had only that same morning given us up for dead. Mo had read the note left by Nick on the big boulder we used as a kitchen. It was clear that Nick thought we were all dead. His note, dated 20 July, read:

Chris sitting it out, battered but not broken, playing the waiting game for a total of five days until Nick arrived with our porters.

Dear all, in the unlikely event of you ever reading this I have gone down to try to catch up with Tut and the porters so that we can come back and look for you. We saw you come down off the mountain on 14 July and assumed you'd be back down the next morning. The porters had already arrived and we had neither the food, nor the money, to keep them. Tut and Aleem therefore went down, with the porters and all the gear, while I waited with six of them to help carry your stuff. I can only assume that something has gone badly wrong.

Tut and I will get back up as quickly as we can.

The note also mentioned that Nick had left the food cache tucked well underneath the big Base Camp boulder with a pile of smaller rocks on top as protection from the bears. We had seen families of brown bears in the distance during the walk along the Biafo. Clive, Chris and Aleem came to within fifty feet of a bear, six feet tall, that stood its ground for ten seconds before it shot off 1,500 feet up steep moraine-covered hillside without effort, before stopping to check on the humans. There had been reports from other expeditions in the area having to curtail their activities due to the bears destroying tents at Base Camp and eating their food supplies while the expeditions were on the mountain.

In the cache we found a tin containing a Purdy fruit cake, powdered milk, sugar and fresh teabags. After tea and cake, Clive, Chris and I collapsed into sleep just before dawn. The next morning the sun shone down on to our wet sleeping bags; I could feel the warmth come right through into the steamy interior. Pulling open the draw cords from inside, poking my head out to see the grass, flowers and the stream, brewing a mug of tea, and feeling the sun burning my skin are beautiful memories I will never lose.

For four days Clive looked after Chris and me, each day hoping for the arrival of porters that Mo should have sent up. In fact, on the fourth day of waiting, we wondered if Mo had fallen down a crevasse on the Biafo Glacier. We were also worried he might have been attacked by bears – perhaps no one knew we were still alive and our families were already grieving for us. The only food we had left were some Tom and Jerry nougat bars, pink in colour and tasting not unlike sweet polystyrene.

With supplies running low and desperate to make contact with the outside world we decided to move on down under our own steam. I made knee pads out of foam sleeping mats; Clive attempted to alleviate some of the pain Chris was suffering by binding his ribs with a shirt. Clive went on down the Baintha Lukpar Glacier to prospect a route that I might manage, while Chris and I packed our rucksacks with the remaining food and a few personal

On the green, green grass that had been our home during the five-day wait for porters. At this point we had faced the possibility that Mo, who had run off down for help, had himself come to grief. We decided to leave and try and make our own way back. Within an hour of starting out Nick and the porters arrived. *Photo:* Chris Bonington.

effects. Realistically, our main hope of survival was in coming across porters by chance or for Clive to go down to Askole as fast as possible. Before we could put this to Clive he was already coming back up with the good news that the Askole porters were on their way.

Mo had, in fact, caught Nick up in Askole after walking continuously, except for catnaps, for a remarkable day and a half. Nick was overwhelmed to hear we were all still alive, as was Tut. Mo had been going for twelve hours when he came across the note left by Nick at Base Camp. Mo had grabbed some cake, a nougat bar and a packet of soup from Nick's food cache and immediately set off for Askole at 5 p.m., desperate to catch up with Nick and Tut before they announced to the world and to our families that we were dead.

The walking distance to Askole from our Base Camp is about thirty miles.

The Biafo Glacier. The edge of the green pasture of Base Camp can be seen just left of the Ogre's Thumb. The porters carried me with difficulty down the Uzun Brakk Glacier to where it meets the Baintha Lukpar, and then more easily down the Biafo to Askole over three days.

Twice Mo fell asleep on his feet to find himself still walking. Sensing danger, he restricted himself to walking for one hour at a time at which point he would take a five-minute catnap. At midnight he could no longer see his way, so he slept for a few hours before stumbling on to arrive in Askole at seven o'clock the next morning. The first person to greet Mo was the headman of the village, Haji Mehdi, whom Mo knew well from previous visits to Trango Tower. Mo was quite overcome: 'The Baltis don't normally show much emotion. But when he saw me he did a sort of vertical take-off into the air, then dashed up and hugged me. Bloody hell, I thought. So I slogged on up the street, very slowly, because it was uphill, and when I came to the camp site there was Nick running towards me. I've never seen such pleasure on a bloke's face. He was convinced we were all dead.' (See *Feeding the Rat*, 2003, Al Alvarez).

12 The Final Stretch

On the fifth morning at Base Camp Nick suddenly arrived with a team of Balti porters and enough poplar wood poles to make a stretcher. As it was being constructed Nick produced, from his rucksack, more food and also some very strong painkillers. All the way down the mountain, to this point, I had no pain relief, in fact we had no first aid kit with us. I had hoped to find at Base Camp at least some relief for my aches and pains but Nick had left nothing of the kind behind; I had a go at him about that which was incredibly insensitive of me after he had just slogged all the way back up to help us.

By midday I was on the stretcher in the midst of the Balti porters carrying me down the steep, and sometimes difficult, moraine-covered Baintha Lukpar Glacier. The Balti were dressed, as always, in their homespun tunics and cotton pantaloons, wearing sawn-off wellingtons and rubber sandals. For the next three days I was surrounded by them as they carried me along so carefully, with Chris walking alongside still coughing and spitting up colourful mucus.

It was a remarkable journey on that home-made stretcher, made up of wooden poles, climbing ropes and sleeping mats. Never once did they look like dropping me and I seldom felt a jolt. It was interesting to lie on the stretcher, listening and waiting, as they made decisions as to which route to take, the pacing of the journey, the choice of camping site, and who would fetch wood, water and stone for their bivouac.

They only seemed to make decisions after a gentle murmur of conversation had gone round the motley band. Perhaps it was the effect of the painkillers putting me on something of a cloud that their voices had blended into a sing-song melody of background sound completely in tune with the rhythm of their village lives. No one ever shouted or became overexcited and neither was there any obvious leader – they seemed to know just what to do and did it in a spirit of cooperation. They were all individualistic, all of them characters in their own right, yet easily capable of working to a common aim in complete accord.

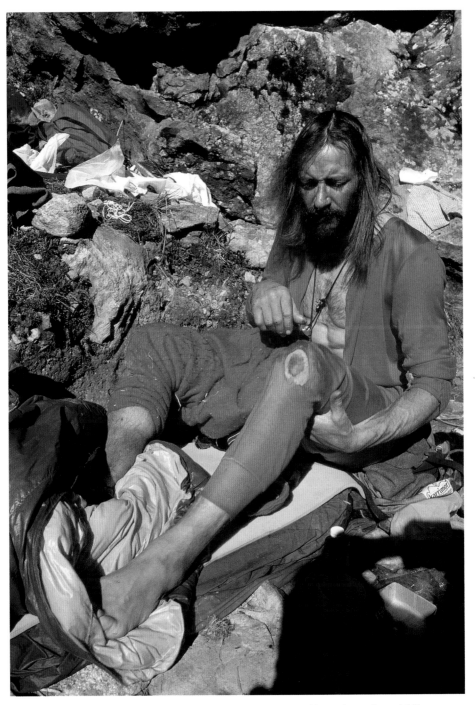

Showing Nick the wounds; with Nick's arrival Chris and I were able to take our first painkilling tablets. We had not packed a first aid kit for the climb. I had worn through four pairs of overtrousers down to my knees, which were more painful than the broken legs at the time. *Photo:* Nick Estcourt.

I could not help speculate that the Balti porters probably thought we were all mad, rushing into their mountains with quite a few of us dying there or being carried or helicoptered out with severe injuries. *Photo:* Clive Rowland.

Over the years I had been pleasantly surprised at the spontaneous generosity of people who had so little, with none of the amenities I take for granted, living on marginal land and whose lives are very much at the mercy of natural processes. Time after time my friends and I had received wonderful hospitality from such people who shared with us what little they had especially when the chips were down. Caring for complete strangers seemed to come so naturally to people living precariously on the edge.

On the fourth day the stretcher party put me down on a flat, well-grazed pasture just before their village of Askole. Within half an hour a helicopter appeared that Mo had arranged; a rather overweight pilot with silver pearl-handled revolvers on each hip stalked across the grass towards me announcing that there was only room for me and no room for Chris or Clive, whose frostbite had become infected. He had brought his batman along for the ride. He said, 'No problem, I will be back in four hours for your friends'. During this announcement and discussion American friends, who had successfully climbed Trango Main Tower, stopped awhile to see how we were and if they could help. I flew off in the helicopter with the reassuring news that Dennis Hennek, who had led the American expedition, John Roskelley and other members of the team would arrange for their two doctors to check out Chris.

Moving down the Biafo Glacier. *Photo:* Clive Rowland.

If, as it seemed, he had pneumonia, they had the means to give him anti-biotics intravenously.

It was a remarkable flight some 1,000 feet up above the Braldu River until we approached the helipad at Skardu. Suddenly there was a clonking noise in the engine which cut out and we dropped the final twenty or so feet without power on to an area of boulders. Although we had been thrown around the cockpit there was no further damage to me or the batman. The pilot however just sat there, ashen – if not green, with beads of sweat pouring down his face, in a state of shock. He said what had happened to the engine just above the ground could so easily have happened when we were 1,000 feet up.

Tut, who had walked out on hearing we were still alive, had been waiting for me and was the first person at the helicopter crash. He went along with me to the hospital where, after X-rays, both my legs were encased in plaster. I was instructed not to put weight on them. The next day I told Tut that I had to get out of the hospital. Tut, who had limped in with a stick said, 'There's only one thing for it – you'll have to get on my back'. Luckily I was by then only skin and bone, well below my usual fighting weight. Tut staggered down the hospital corridor almost bent double with my weight – on either side were amputees missing arms and some devoid of both legs.

On the thirteenth day after the accident Chris and I reached Askole. *Photo:* Clive Rowland.

The crashed helicopter wasn't going anywhere for a long time – there was a problem. In fact, it was to be seven more days before Chris could be brought out. He had spent the most frustrating week, staying in a dusty adobe house, thinking he had been abandoned, listening day after day for the noise of the helicopter, which never came. Everyone else had left, expecting Chris to be flying overhead at any time. He was visited by the two American doctors from the Trango Tower expedition who diagnosed and treated Chris for pneumonia. In total frustration Chris began to walk out and, of course, that same morning the helicopter appeared overhead at first unable to locate him.

Once in the helicopter Chris persuaded the pilot to take him direct to Islamabad and drop him near the British embassy. The most suitable place was a large international golf course where he was deposited. The helicopter flew off leaving Chris, totally emaciated, dusty, dirty and unwashed, with his bags at his side on the eighteenth green. He walked across to the clubhouse in his filthy red long johns, vest, with one arm in a sling, his beard and hair in a tangle. People backed away at the sight but eventually he got on to the telephone and Caroline, our embassy hostess, arrived to pick Chris up and take him away to the comforts within the embassy compound.

Chris arrived back at the embassy on 5 August where he met Clive and Steph as they were preparing to drive all the gear home. A few hours later

Within half an hour of reaching Askole a helicopter came, but unfortunately could only take one person since the pilot had brought along his batman. The helicopter crash-landed well before the helipad at Skardu.

Nick also arrived – he and Aleem had been stuck in Skardu with all the remaining gear. Nick had got it out just in time to pack it into the white van.

By 4 August, three weeks and one day after the accident, I was being plastered and pinned in Nottingham General Hospital. Tut, Mo and Jackie were also back in Britain. Chris flew out on 7 August, and finally, Nick, who – frustratingly – could not get a flight home until 12 August. Our little band of brothers on the mountain had shown what could be done in a crisis by a small team, isolated, cut off from the outside world, in some ways like a commando unit behind enemy lines, but in our case without radios or any other communication devices. Chris, Clive and Mo had got me with my two broken legs down the steepest part of the mountain. After Chris smashed his ribs on the Red Pillar, Mo and Clive worked tirelessly to get both of us down from 22,000 feet to the glacier. It was all done in a totally competent and controlled manner, thanks to their wide mountaineering experience, and natural humanity to stay and put it into practice. For eight days, from the accident down to Base Camp, I was looked after and cared for with total attention during the day and throughout the night. I doubt if any climbers in our position could have been in better hands. These two confirmed amateurs did a totally professional job in getting us down and out from the Ogre.

No single person did more for the overall success of the expedition, and getting us home again, than Nick. I cannot think of anyone more diligent; right from the start he took it upon himself to take charge of the food and the finances throughout the expedition, spending hours changing money in banks and haggling with porters over their pay. He had taken on most of the cooking at Base Camp. For someone who wanted to return home after his climb up to the West Summit it was a strange irony that it was Nick who had to wait patiently for our return, increasingly thinking we were all dead, and would have to announce this fact to our wives and families.

Nick had begun to fret about our fate from 16 July onwards, becoming ever more worried as the days passed until, by 22 July, he was convinced that we were all dead. This would have been a trial for anyone but especially for someone who was so conscientious. The awful thing is simply not knowing and agonising over likely scenarios, which is what Nick did. His diary records the thoughts churning around in his head: 'All four down in a windslab avalanche, a multiple accident on a fixed rope.' He was constantly vigilant on the mountain, peering through his binoculars, 'Every stone on the glacier seemed to move … if you listened hard enough you can hear human voices

Left: Chris was stuck in Askole for seven more days before another helicopter could be found. Luckily he was treated for pneumonia by the American Trango Tower expedition doctors, who gave him antibiotics intravenously. *Photo:* Dennis Hennek.

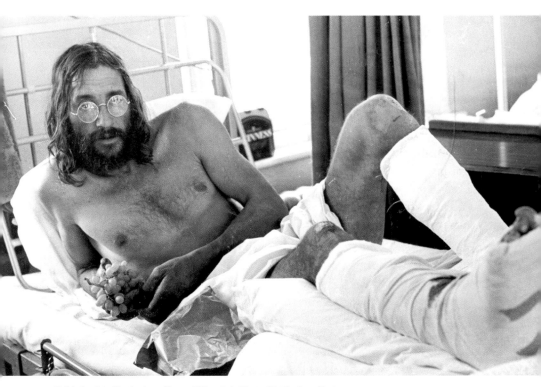

Safely back in Nottingham General Hospital. *Photo: Nottingham Post.*

in the sound of running water or falling stone'. And in another entry: 'Hardly slept a wink, thought I saw a green flare up on the glacier – also a distinct shout of "Nick" – no further sounds though!'

Nick commented how incredibly fast things can change. After a final bad night, 'no sleep – worried – how to break it to Jackie and Steph', then Mo comes into Askole at 9 a.m. to such huge relief for Nick and Tut; Tut, who for many days had been holed up in a house in Askole reading books and resting his aching leg.

On the way back up with the porters on 22 July Nick nearly drowned after losing his footing while crossing a river near Mango; he was being swept away when a porter waded in, supported by his stick, and pulled him out, probably saving his life. That night the porters lit a big fire to dry his clothes. They too had recognised in Nick a selfless mountain man and took him under their wing.

I was well looked after in Nottingham General Hospital, with friends arriving from near and far, loaded with goodies of all kinds. Pete Minks brought a six-pack of Guinness from Liverpool and Jan came in twice a day with good home-cooked food as the hospital mashed potato and cabbage were of the same colour, and the meat was grey and tough as old boots.

Mr Mulholland, the surgeon, well regarded in the East Midlands, gave me confidence before the operation by telling me that he had treated similar injuries amongst coal miners who had been extricated from a collapsed coal seam.

The impact had broken the end of the tibia and also split it some way up its length. The other leg was cracked above the ankle without being displaced. Three weeks after the accident, the surgeon put it all back together again with the help of four rather long screws – stainless steel of course, only the best from Nottingham General. I asked Mr Mulholland whether the healing process had begun and he said that indeed there were signs that the surfaces of the bone at the fractures were beginning to fuse but were still rather like wet cement. Mr Mulholland was easily able to manoeuvre the parts back together and clean up broken cartilage before sewing and plastering me up. He said that if it had been left another week he would have had to rebreak the ankle.

I therefore made the mental note not to leave any future fractures too long before seeing the surgeon. I tried to keep fit in the hospital doing pull-ups and press-ups but it soon became obvious that I would have to cancel the expedition to Nuptse I was planning for the autumn. By mid October I went out into Derbyshire with Tim Lewis for a first post-op climb. I followed Tim up *Suicide Wall* on Cratcliffe Tor without too many aches and pains. By late November I had recovered enough to play my first post-op game of rugby for the Nottingham Moderns.

As with most injuries to joints we inflict upon ourselves when young, they do tend to catch up with you in later life. In my case I subsequently had the screws removed and the ankle fused in 2015 as the joint had become arthritic. Unfortunately, it became infected and I developed septicaemia which entailed another ten days in hospital being fed antibiotics intravenously. For the last two years the ankle has recovered and allowed me to continue hillwalking and gentle rock climbing.

As for the climb, looking back, I can see that after Everest I thought I was invincible, that I could do anything. I was far too arrogant believing in my own myth. There comes a time when a man's got to do what a man's got to do. Sometimes he does it gently, feeling his way, sometimes he goes at it like a bull at a gate and that's when he gets hurt. On Everest, Dougal and I climbed with great circumspection, caring for each other as we proceeded with humility to the summit. On the Ogre I was far too gung-ho. I remember standing at the bottom before going up for the final attempt, saying to myself as I looked up at it, 'Right, I'm going to get this body from this grass to the top of that mountain whatever happens'. After all the energy I had expended in getting to the base of the mountain during the recce, organising things

Back home from hospital with Martha and Jan.

back in Nottingham, then sitting around waiting for Tut's leg to heal, I had built up, like Chris, a head of steam for the climb, boiling over with curiosity to know the lie of the land up there and how I would cope on steep rock at 23,000 feet.

An interesting postscript to our expedition was that the route was almost repeated. In 1978 the Shizuoka Tohan Club, then under the leadership of Yukio Katsumi, returned to rechallenge the South Face after being avalanched off in 1974. His team members were Kimio Itokawa, Shiro Aoki, Tetsuji Furuta, Toshiro Kitamura, Shosaku Kato and Masanobu Yonezawa.

The first we knew of this was when we received a cassette of used film, taken by Chris that he had left in his rucksack, and found by the Japanese about 200 feet below the summit. According to the account in the *Iwa To Yuki*, February 1979, three of the team – Katsumi, Itokawa and Kitamura – had a real struggle to climb the final overhang. They managed to surmount it but were so drained they retreated only ten metres from the summit. 'They were satisfied only to climb the South Face of "Ogre" without accident.'

Nearly a quarter of a century elapsed between the first ascent in 1977 and the second in 2001. Despite many attempts, including one by French climbers Michel Fauquet and Vincent Vine, who climbed the South Pillar to the upper snowfields in 1983, nobody reached the summit for twenty-four years.

In 2001 Thomas Huber from Bavaria and two Swiss friends, Iwan Wolf and Urs Stöcker, succeeded in making the sixth ascent of the South Pillar. They then went on to climb the South Face snowfields and after a total of two weeks of climbing reached the summit early on 22 July. Thomas later came to Cumbria to interview and film Chris and me, to give the film his team had made of their climb a historical perspective. It was only then when reliving the expedition, and in particular the climb up, that we fully appreciated what an interesting climb it was. The whole expedition had been dominated in our minds by the epic descent.

Thomas said that, in his opinion, after doing some research, that what we had achieved on the final tower was the hardest climbing ever done at the time at that altitude. That was good to hear, but I should add that Thomas and his friends climbed in wild and windy weather whereas for Chris and me there wasn't a breath of wind blowing over the rough red granite of the summit tower.

The third ascent of the Ogre was made in 2012 by a new route and for the first time in brilliant alpine style by the Americans, Hayden Kennedy and Kyle Dempster. They left their Base Camp on the Choktoi Glacier on 18 August accompanied by Josh Wharton until he was stopped by altitude sickness at the last bivouac. They followed a circuitous line up the south side of the mountain on snow, ice and difficult rock to reach the summit on 21 August. They all arrived safely back at Base Camp on 23 August after six days of inspired route finding and hard climbing thirty-five years after the first ascent. For this impeccably executed climb they received a Piolet d'Or in 2013.

Afterword

There was another interesting matter arising from the post-expedition media aspect, as Al Alvarez wrote in his semi-autobiography of himself and biography of Mo, *Feeding the Rat*: 'Between the rescue, and the ensuing publicity, a curious conjuring trick took place. Mo and Rowland effectively vanished from the story.' In all the media hype Mo and Clive were hardly mentioned since Fleet Street were only interested in big names. Mo was, after all, only human, so even if he did have a distaste for publicity, he would naturally have preferred the whole story to be told. He did write a humorous article for the *Alpine Journal* in a typically self-deprecating and understated fashion as if to drive home his feelings. In just a few lines about his part in the retreat from the Ogre he wrote, 'Strangely enough it was not a frightening experience and while not pleasurable, it certainly did not lack in excitement'.

Dougal, Tut and I had the north buttress of Nuptse in Nepal booked for the autumn of 1977, but with Dougal's death, and then my two broken legs and Tut's seriously injured thigh we abandoned our plan, having only one good leg between us. I had sent the Nepali Ministry of Tourism all the information about our epics on the Ogre including press reports with a photograph showing me in Nottingham General Hospital with both legs in plaster, hoping it would impress them enough to carry our application and the royalty payment over to 1978. The only reply I got was, 'your request is not possible, please make every effort to carry out your obligations in future when booking peaks in Nepal'. Wonderful people, bureaucrats. We ground our teeth and rebooked for the autumn of 1978.

Tut's leg was slow to heal – it remained stiff and very painful. He was advised by his doctors to seek treatment with the local Saddleworth physio-therapist, Mary Hall. During the following weeks his leg improved and his love life flourished thanks to meeting Mary's daughter, Jane, with whom he has lived happily ever after.

Left: K2, the next objective. *Photo:* Nick Estcourt.

The water supply has come off fields fertilised with animal and human excrement. It is then used for all domestic requirements: washing, drinking and cooking. This is the main reason that up until 1990 child mortality was over fifty per cent, mainly from diarrhoea and enteritis.

Chris appeared on television several times a day during the winter, between programmes, informing the viewers how on the Ogre, 'We boiled up snow and ice to make hot strong Bovril to thaw ourselves out. And how that beefy taste cheered us.' Full-page advertisements saying the same appeared in the tabloid press ingraining Chris on the national consciousness and bringing the Ogre into the public domain.

I was to make eight visits to Pakistan altogether. After the Ogre there were four expeditions to K2, all of them fraught with difficulty and danger. On the first visit to K2 in 1978 we lost Nick Estcourt in an avalanche when trying to make a new route up the West Ridge, but that is another story to be included in a forthcoming book about K2.

The last visit I made to Pakistan was to the Latok mountains in 1990 where one of our porters tripped and fell with his expedition load into the Braldu River never to be seen again. We spent three days in Askole awaiting a police patrol to come down from the hills so we could obtain a death certificate that would help claim the insurance on behalf of the porter's family.

During our stay we discovered that there was over fifty per cent child mortality, mainly due to diarrhoea and enteritis. The women were taking water for all domestic purposes – drinking, washing, cooking – from an intermittent stream that ran down the main lane of the village several times a day when released from irrigating the fields. The crops were nourished with

All's well that ends well.

animal and also human excrement so the source of this problem was not hard to identify. The cause of the main health problem was, as in Victorian Britain, polluted water. I decided I would do something about it; I was in fact quite angry that in this day and age there was such unnecessary suffering.

The village people of Askole had done so much for me in making ascents of their mountains possible, not to mention rescuing me from the Ogre, that it only seemed right to help out. There was a clear freshwater stream less than a mile away gurgling out of the hillside all year round. I made contact with the excellent Aga Khan Rural Support Programme in Skardu who eventually brought spring water by pipe buried three feet down against the winter cold to seventeen standpipes around the village. Within just a few years so many more children were reaching the age of five. The fact that I had climbed Everest and had now broken my legs on the Ogre, gave me a high enough profile to raise the $10,000 this project cost. I should say that $5,000 of this was generously donated via Jed Williams from the American Alpine Club. This was the project that gave me the confidence to react positively to requests in Nepal to put in schools, health posts and porter shelters as well as pipes for clean water. So indirectly from the drama on the Ogre, and the ensuing publicity, we were able to set up Community Action Nepal which now supports over fifty projects in Nepal.

Acknowledgements

This book has been written in three months so everyone who contributed did so at short notice, none more so than Anne Manger who typed it up either directly from my handwritten pencilled scrawl or more usually from my reading from notes. This dictation often took place at weekends via the telephone. Anne also cancelled appointments to transcribe Mo's audio tapes that suddenly turned up during the later stages of this book. Occasionally when Anne was busy CAN's UK office manager, Ruth Moore, stood in dealing with correspondence with those who offered discerning comments.

After a thorough proofread of the text, Di Stubbs gave invaluable and much-appreciated comment throughout the book. Catherine Moorehead, the biographer of Henry Haversham Godwin-Austen, lived up to her reputation as a meticulous researcher, as I know from her rapid response to my requests to collaborate on solving the mystery of the positioning and naming of the Ogre/Baintha Brakk.

Professor Mikel Vause of Weber State University, Utah, literary critic Noel Dawson and Stephen Goodwin, former editor of the *Alpine Journal,* also contributed hugely to the overall sense of the book. Oxford University Professor of Earth Sciences Mike Searle helped knock into shape the origins of the Karakoram and therefore the Ogre. Tamotsu [Tom] Nakamura, the prolific explorer of East Tibet, and his fellow countryman, Kinichi Yamamori, chairman of the Himalayan Association of Japan, helped with information on the important Japanese expeditions to the Ogre. Nazir Sabir, ex-minister of education for Hunza, and Muhammad Iqbal from Askole, helped shed light on the naming of the Ogre as Baintha Brakk. Morag MacDonald from the Falconer Museum in Forres should also be thanked for trying to track down the extent of Hugh Falconer's explorations. Brian Scott, Phil Powell and especially the forensic Sarah Loving spotted grammatical and factual errors. Salman Rashid, author of *The Apricot Road to Yarkand* (2011), has also contributed to the interpretation of the name Baintha Brakk and when the name Ogre was first used.

The story of our climb was helped enormously by Caroline Estcourt allowing me access to Nick's diary of the expedition. I am also grateful to Kelda Roe of Mountain Heritage Trust, the archivist and keeper of this diary, for actually transcribing it. For the same reason I am most grateful to Clive and Fiona Rowland for allowing me to see Clive's memoirs in draft, and also to Clive, as well as Tut Braithwaite, for checking on the accuracy of my text. Just as I had completed the book, Jackie Anthoine discovered in her loft six reels of Super 8 film with a few supporting cassette tapes that Mo had put together forty years ago. Jackie allowed me to use this material, with discretion, and I am very grateful for her permission as it has added much to the story.

The images form a vital part of this book and I therefore thank, most sincerely, Clive and Chris Bonington for allowing me to use their photographs taken on the expedition, and also Caroline Estcourt for the use of Nick's images. Christine Gee, Glyn Hughes, Denise Prior and Peter Rowland, Honorary Keeper of the Alpine Club's photographs, all helped make available historical images. David Nightingale laboriously prepared all images for the book.

I thank Jon Barton, the founder of Vertebrate, and his team, who took over the edit, design, production and printing of the book in Vertebrate's usual professional manner.

Last, but not least, I must thank Trish my wonderful wife who every day these last three months has been there to comment as I wrote, and drastically reduce domestic pressures to make life more conducive to writing. Trish also had to cope with my tendency to be writing by 4 a.m., morning after morning.

Further Reading

Alvarez, Al, *Feeding the Rat* (London: Bloomsbury, 2003).

Bonington, Chris, *Mountaineer* (Sheffield: Vertebrate Publishing, 2016).
— *The Everest Years* (Sheffield: Vertebrate Publishing, 2017).

Bruce, Hon. C.G., *Himalayan Wanderer* (London: Alexander Maclehose, 1934).

Conway, W.M., *Climbing and Exploration in the Karakoram-Himalayas* (London: T. Fisher Unwin, 1894).

Dalrymple, William, *The Last Mughal* (London: Bloomsbury, 2006).

Goodwin, Buster, *Life Among the Pathans* (Rawalpindi: Ferozsons of Rawalpindi, 1975).

Keay, John, *When Men & Mountains Meet* (London: John Murray, 1977).

Longstaff, Tom, *This My Voyage* (London: John Murray, 1950).

Mason, Kenneth, *Abode of Snow* (London: Diadem Books, 1987).

Moorehead, Catherine, *The K2 Man (and his Molluscs)* (Glasgow: The In Pinn, 2013).

Pauly, Thomas H., *Game Faces* (Lincoln & London: University of Nebraska Press, 2012).

Russell, Scott, *Mountain Prospect* (London: Chatto & Windus, 1946).

Scott, Doug, *Himalayan Climber* (London: Bâton Wicks, 1994).
— *Up and About* (Sheffield: Vertebrate Publishing, 2015).

Searle, Mike, *Colliding Continents* (Oxford: Oxford University Press, 2013).

Shaw, Isobel and Ben, *Pakistan Trekking Guide* (Hong Kong: Odyssey, 1993).

Shipton, Eric, *Blank on the Map* (Sheffield: Vertebrate Digital, 2014).
— *That Untravelled World* (Sheffield: Vertebrate Publishing, 2017).

Vigne, Godfrey, *Travels in Kashmir* (London: Henry Colburn, 1842).

Wells, Colin, *Who's Who in British Climbing* (Buxton: The Climbing Company Limited, 2008).

Workman, Fanny Bullock, and William Hunter, *The Call of the Snowy Hispar* (London: Constable and Company Ltd, 1910).

Younghusband, Francis, *The Heart of a Continent* (London: John Murray, 1937).

The Author

Doug Scott (b.1941). I had the confidence to launch this expedition to the rocky Ogre peak with Clive Rowland because I had steadily, over the previous fifteen years, spent a good deal of time climbing steep rock with members of the Nottingham Climbers' Club. In the 1960s we climbed the North-East Face of the Piz Badile, the north faces of the Tre Cime in the Dolomites, and the classic rock climbs of the Western Alps including the Bonatti Pillar on the Dru and the West Face of the Aiguille de Blaitière. In 1970 we went over to Norway, climbing a number of classic routes around Andalsnes including the highest big wall in Europe, the Troll Wall, in seventeen hours of climbing.

In 1971 I climbed for six weeks in Yosemite Valley in California, including 3,500 feet up the *Salathé Wall* on El Capitan with Peter Habeler. I returned to America in 1973 to climb the *Nose* of El Cap with Rick White, taking five days in an effort to climb it as freely as possible. Also during the 1970s I organised four rock climbing expeditions to Baffin Island. In 1972 I climbed the 5,000-foot East Pillar of Mount Asgard, right on the Arctic Circle.

I also managed to organise several small overland expeditions to the Tibesti Mountains of Chad, Kurdistan and the Hindu Kush where we climbed the South Face of Koh-i-Bandaka (22,470 feet/6,850 metres) in alpine style. In the 1970s I was also invited on three expeditions to the South-West Face of Everest, eventually climbing to the summit in 1975 with Dougal Haston.

Somehow or other over the years I managed to go on more than forty expeditions to the high mountains of Asia and many other mountain ranges. For about twenty years I was totally obsessed with mountains and going off with the boys climbing. As I became old and feeble I directed my energies towards helping the people in Nepal, who had helped me climb their mountains, by building schools, health posts and porter rescue shelters. With the help of equally enthusiastic trustees and some 100-odd volunteers in Britain, Community Action Nepal has now set up and continues to support over fifty projects.

Photo: Geoff Beatty.

In 1994 I was made a CBE and in 1999 awarded the Patron's Medal of the Royal Geographical Society. I was most proud to be president of the Alpine Club from 1999 to 2001 and it was a great honour to receive the Lifetime Achievement Award from the Piolets d'Or in 2011 following on from Walter Bonatti and Reinhold Messner.

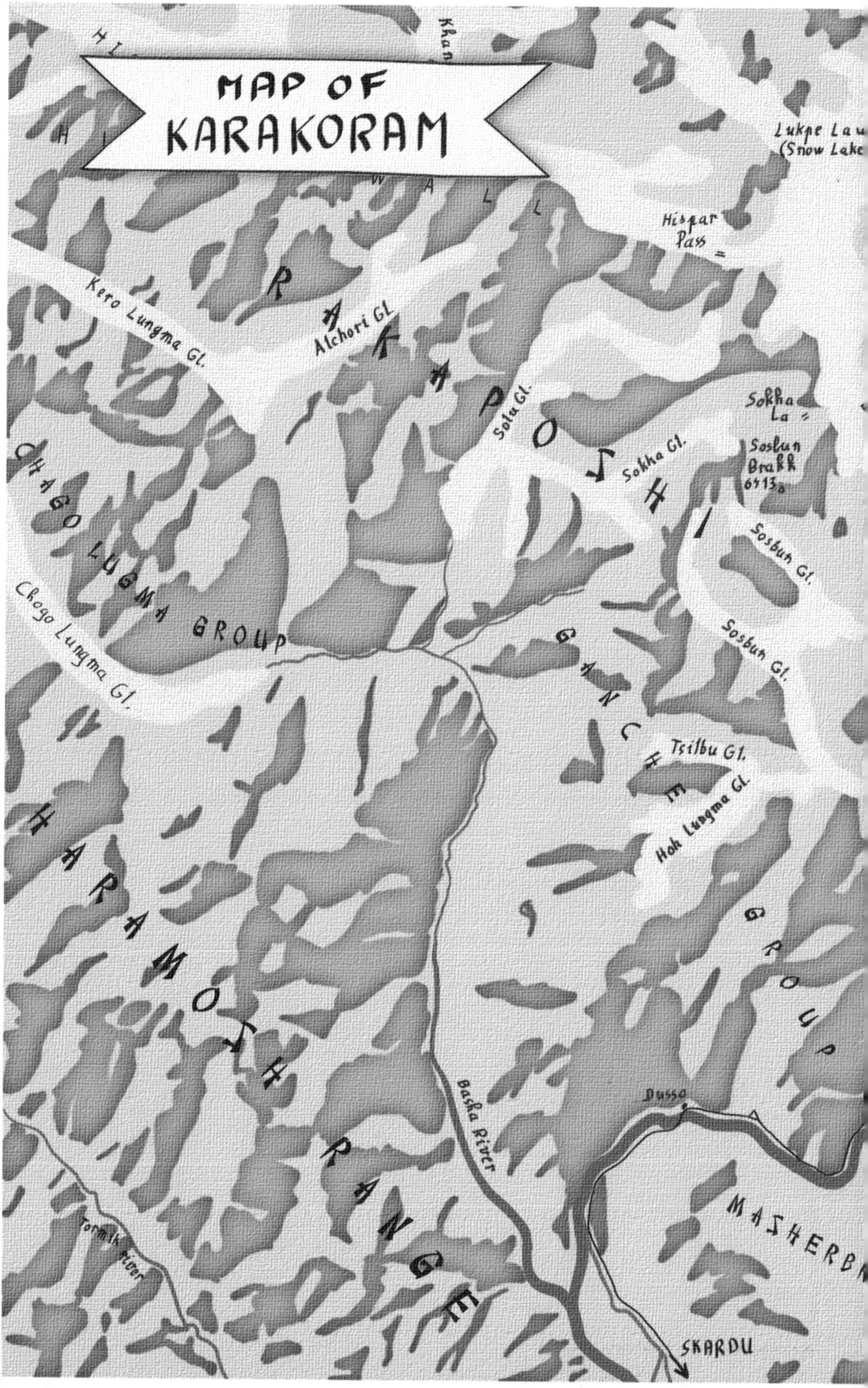

MAP OF KARAKORAM

HIMALAYA WALL

Khan

Lukpe La
(Snow Lake)

Hispar Pass

KARAKORAM

Kero Lungma Gl.

Alchori Gl.

Solu Gl.

Sokha La

Sokha Gl.

Soslun Brakk 6413

RAKAPOSHI

Sosbun Gl.

Sosbun Gl.

Chogo Lungma Group

Chogo Lungma Gl.

GANCHEM

Tsilbu Gl.

Hoh Lungma Gl.

GROUP

HARAMOSH RANGE

Basha River

Dusso

Tormik River

MASHERB

SKARDU